Who Is Bob_34?

Who Is Bob_34?

Investigating Child Cyberpornography

Francis Fortin and Patrice Corriveau
Translated by Käthe Roth

UBCPress · Vancouver · Toronto

Originally published in French as *Cyberpédophiles et autres agresseurs sexuels*
© 2011, VLB éditeur, division du Groupe Sogides Inc.

23 22 21 20 19 18 17 16 15   5 4 3 2 1

Printed in Canada on FSC-certified ancient-forest-free paper
(100% post-consumer recycled) that is processed chlorine- and acid-free.

ISBN 978-0-7748-2967-0 (bound); — ISBN 978-0-7748-2968-7 (pbk.); —
ISBN 978-0-7748-2969-4 (pdf); — ISBN 978-0-7748-2970-0 (epub)

Cataloguing-in-publication data for this book is available from Library and Archives
Canada.

Canadä

UBC Press gratefully acknowledges the financial support for our publishing program
of the Government of Canada (through the Canada Book Fund), the Canada Council
for the Arts, and the British Columbia Arts Council.

We acknowledge the financial support of the Government of Canada, through the
National Translation Program for Book Publishing for our translation activities.

UBC Press
The University of British Columbia
2029 West Mall
Vancouver, BC V6T 1Z2
www.ubcpress.ca

Contents

Who Is Bob_34?

Introduction

Every day, eye-catching headlines such as "International live-streamed pedophile ring busted by authorities,"[1] "Alarming growth in trafficking of child pornography on the Internet,"[2] and "Vast network of pedophiles dismantled, leading to the arrests of 348 individuals worldwide"[3] explode in the media, giving the impression that the Internet is awash with perverts. It is easy to believe that an ever-growing number of child-pornography collectors and potential rapists are lurking in cyberspace, ready to pounce on victims made accessible through the social proximity facilitated by the virtual universe. Some even wonder if the Internet has somehow created new pedophiles.[4]

Some commentators claim that the Internet has become the prime vector of expansion for the sex industry, especially for child pornography (Legardinier 2002, 22). Statistical observations on the scope of the phenomenon abound. As far back as 1998, only a few years after the Internet boom began, the Canadian Police College estimated that more than a million sexually explicit photographs featuring children had been posted on the Internet.[5] In April 2000, UNICEF declared that a search conducted using Google, one of the most popular search engines on the web, had turned up more than 450,000 child-pornography sites.[6] The previous year, Cyberangels, an online education and security program, listed 30,000 pedophilia sites out of some 4.3 million (Guttman 1999). In 2004, the Reuters news agency, in an article citing data from the Italian association Rainbow

Phone, informed its readers that "the number of pedophilia Web sites grew by 70% in 2003" and noted that "17,016 Web sites whose content included pornographic representations involving children were reported to national and international authorities last year, notably to the FBI and Interpol."[7] A closer look shows, however, that it was not the number of sites but the number of denunciations of these sites that had grown. In 2009, the United Nations' Special Rapporteur on the Sale of Children, Child Prostitution and Child Pornography noted, "The United Nations Children's Fund (UNICEF) estimates that there are more than 4 million sites featuring victims who are young minors."[8] Ethel Quayle and Terry Jones (2011, 11) found that in 2011 the ChildBase of the Child Exploitation and Online Protection Centre in Great Britain had 807,525 unique images. In Canada, research by the Canadian Centre for Child Protection listed 15,662 websites hosting images of child sexual abuse between September 26, 2002, and March 31, 2009 (Bunzeluk 2009).

The only conclusion that we can draw from this mixed bag of statistics is that although the phenomenon is of concern, it is impossible to obtain an accurate and empirically verified picture of its scope, as approximations vary widely. Some rightly point out that these figures, even if not precise, do indicate a trend. However, a closer look shows that these statistics not only are approximations but also conflate adult pornography and child pornography, even though these two subjects are distinct, as pornography featuring adults is legal, but child pornography is not.

A review of the scholarly literature reveals that some researchers indeed conflate child cyberpornography with other issues, such as adult pornography, obscenity, human trafficking, sexual assault, and even prostitution, both adult and child. For instance, Poulin (2004, 184; our translation) notes, in a subsection of his book devoted to child pornography, "According to research conducted at the University of Pennsylvania, between 300,000 and 400,000 children in the United States are forced into prostitution, pornography, or other forms of sexual exploitation each year." Although these subjects overlap occasionally, it is imprudent to combine them under the pretext that they are simply variants of what is commonly called the sex trade, or to suggest that participation in one of these activities will sooner or later lead the individuals involved to engage in other, even more high-risk practices – for example, that adult pornography will lead to child pornography, which will lead eventually to sexual assault.

What is more, the media (and certain "experts") too often accentuate the scope of the phenomenon without supplying the necessary details, notably by omitting to mention the numerous methodological limitations inherent to such assessments, as few empirical studies use first-hand data. The very notion of quantitatively assessing the number of child-pornography images in cyberspace poses a problem in terms of the validity of sources. On the one hand, the means of producing and distributing child pornography are in constant evolution; on the other hand, exchanges of this type of material take place essentially within very clandestine circles, beyond the view of researchers and even the police. Thus, it is impossible to say whether the images listed in official assessments represent the tip of the iceberg or the sum total. Finally, as we will see, there is no real consensus among experts when it comes to determining the exact definition of a child-pornography image (Quayle and Taylor 2002).

Let us take the example of Canada. Section 163.1(1) of the Canadian Criminal Code prohibits all photographic, film, video, or other representation, produced by mechanical or electronic means, of persons younger than eighteen years of age "the dominant characteristic of which is the depiction, for a sexual purpose, of a sexual organ or the anal region." In its *Sharpe* ruling, however, the Supreme Court of Canada specified,

> An objective approach must be applied to the terms "dominant characteristic" and "for a sexual purpose." The question is whether a reasonable viewer, looking at the depiction objectively and in context, would see its "dominant characteristic" as the depiction of the child's sexual organ or anal region in a manner that is reasonably perceived as intended to cause sexual stimulation to some viewers.[9]

Yet expressions such as "reasonable viewer," "in context," "reasonably perceived," and "some viewers" are themselves open to interpretation. Reactions to the 1999 Calvin Klein ad campaign for children's underwear illustrate the extent to which judgments concerning what is and is not pornographic are variable and open to debate: many Americans deemed the photograph of two young children playing on a couch in their underwear unacceptable because it might have, in their view, encouraged pedophile impulses, whereas others considered the uproar silly.

Other countries, such as Canada, France, and Switzerland, do not consider portrayals of a naked or undressed child in an appropriate context (swimming pool, beach, bath, etc.) illicit. In Swiss legal doctrine, material that "has the goal of sexual excitement highlighting the genitals of children, provocative poses, or sexually explicit positions" is pedo-pornographic

(Action Innocence 2008; our translation). Once again, there is room for interpretation, which indicates that divergences will appear whenever a determination is to be made about whether a particular photograph should be added to the list of pedo-pornographic images.

There is no doubt, however, that the number of child-pornography images available in cyberspace has risen constantly since the blossoming of the Internet in the mid-1990s. With their accessibility and wide variety of means of communication, information and communications technologies (ICTs) facilitate and accentuate the production, distribution, and exchange of files containing child pornography. Pedo-pornographic materials take many forms – photographs, videos, and text messages, as well as real-time webcam images[10] – and can now transit simultaneously via the web, email, electronic bulletin boards, chat rooms, peer-to-peer technologies, and newsgroup and discussion forums. Each ICT is different: some offer public access, whereas others are private and secret.[11]

The plurality of means of communication forces researchers to formulate research protocols adapted to each of them, with all of the difficulties that this may entail. Legal constraints may also limit, or even dissuade, independent researchers, as section 163.1(4.1) of the Canadian Criminal Code forbids even accessing material containing child pornography. These legal constraints, added to the numerous difficulties inherent to the study of ICTs, have certainly discouraged many, and this is no doubt the reason for which studies based on primary data are still fragmentary and rare.

Fortunately, a provision of the Canadian Criminal Code, section 163.1(3), states, "No person shall be convicted of an offence under this section if the acts that are alleged to constitute the offence serve the public good and do not extend beyond what serves the public good." The notion of "public good" is interpreted by the Supreme Court of Canada in the *Sharpe* ruling as what is "necessary or advantageous ... to the administration of justice, the pursuit of science." In other words, "Examples of possession of child pornography which could serve the public good include possession of child pornography by people in the justice system for purposes associated with prosecution, by researchers studying the effects of exposure to child pornography, and by those in possession of works addressing the political or philosophical aspects of child pornography." In fact, all of our research presented in this volume was conducted on the premises and under the supervision of officers of the Sûreté du Québec's technological crime squad, and it could not have been undertaken without their support. We would like to thank them, once again, for their trust and open-mindedness.

This book is the result of a number of years of work, during which much of our time was spent reading, thinking about, and conducting research projects on different themes related to child pornography in cyberspace. As our investigations advanced, we became increasingly aware of the complexity of the phenomenon, the limited number of empirical studies on the subject, and, above all, the limits to what we could uncover given the time and the means available to us.

Thus, we make absolutely no claim to having answered all of the questions linked to the multiple facets of this illicit ICT-mediated trade.[12] The more modest objectives of this book are to present a general overview of scholarly knowledge on the complex issue of child pornography, and to add to or enrich this knowledge with our empirical studies using primary data.

We therefore felt the need to paint as fair a portrait as possible of the state of knowledge on the subject, even if this meant challenging certain preconceptions. With this in mind, research protocols were formulated to deal with specific aspects related to this social issue. The themes addressed in this book are quite independent of one another because they refer to specific research areas. Of course, the book has an overall coherence and logical sequence, but a reader may well skip a chapter temporarily to go to another one.

By its very nature, cyberspace is a plural and vast world that can be intimidating to the neophyte. To provide some context, the first three chapters of this book give an overview of the trade in child pornography. In Chapter 1, we explain the role played by the Sûreté du Québec's technological crime squad in hunting down individuals who exchange and collect illicit images, and we clarify certain legal points, including what Canadian law says about child pornography, how the illegality of pornography is established, and why it is so difficult to establish a standard definition of child pornography at the international level. We give a brief history of the evolution of ICTs and how they have impacted the production and distribution of child pornography in Chapter 2. Finally, in Chapter 3, we discuss the nature and quantity of the content found in the computers of collectors and in cyberspace, and we examine who the victims portrayed in these images are.

In Chapters 4 and 5, we delve more deeply into the modus operandi of child-pornography collectors in their search for new materials. First, we try to understand why, contrary to popular opinion, websites are not cyberpedophiles' primary source of child-pornography images. More specifically, we explore the use of the Google and Yahoo search engines to find child pornography on the web. The objective of Chapter 4 thus is not to look at the availability and quantity of illicit images on the Internet, which is a foregone conclusion. Rather, we want to determine whether it is easy for an average user – a web surfer who uses mainly traditional search engines, as the vast majority do – to obtain child pornography on the web.

This leads us, in Chapter 5, to discuss the variety of communications that take place in Usenet newsgroups, which are less well known to the general public. We infiltrated three child-pornography newsgroups to examine the nature of the social connections that are woven within these virtual communities. We discovered, among other things, that virtual identities do not impede the formation of a community based on mutual assistance, cooperation, and the sharing of deviant values. In this regard, we analyze which forms of solidarity (technical, emotional, and so on) are formed. What rules govern the members of this community? Do conflicts break out among these virtual users, as happens in all social groups? How do the members ensure the survival and security of their community? To answer these questions, we analyzed more than sixteen hundred text messages written by child-pornography consumers and collectors.

In our final chapter, we analyze the profile of child-pornography collectors arrested in Quebec, Canada, and the United States. Who are these cyberpedophiles? What are their sociodemographic characteristics? Do they have things in common, and if they do, what are they? Is it possible to paint one or more standard portraits of these people, and do some of them present a higher risk of taking action? Are they different in this from past generations of pedophiles? What is the link between the viewing of child pornography and the sexual abuse of children? In short, how have the emergence of the Internet and the proliferation of ICTs changed the game? We conclude by suggesting some future directions for research on the trade in child pornography in the digital age.

1

The Investigators and the Law

To fight against new forms of criminality in the virtual world, governments have formed specialized units that both uncover cyberpedophiles and keep track of individuals who use ICTs to commit crimes of all types. Most units were formed following the attacks of 9/11, when law enforcement and legislators realized that they had to know more about criminals' use of these technologies, as the al-Qaeda operatives had used text messaging systems to plan their attacks (Gagnon 2007). In October 2001, the Sûreté du Québec created a unit with the specific mandate of analyzing complaints concerning cybercrime. The unit was to assist the force's officers and support municipal police forces that did not have the resources necessary to investigate this often complex type of criminal activity. A few years later, the Ministère de la Sécurité publique confirmed that the cybersurveillance mandate belonged to the Sûreté du Québec (Ministère de la Sécurité publique du Québec 2007). The cybersurveillance unit was given the mission of instituting a structure to monitor criminal activities taking place on the Internet, keep up to date on new technologies, collect information, and share this information (via strategic and tactical analysis reports) with all stakeholders concerned with cybercrime (Ouellet 2008). It was in the context of these research activities that we met to work on the issue of child pornography in cyberspace.

Although the Internet surveillance unit is mandated to respond to all cases of crimes in which a computer is used as an object or a tool, the investigators estimate that about 75 percent of their time is devoted to looking into the sexual exploitation of children on the Internet – that is, child pornography, Internet child luring, and child prostitution using ICTs. It is important to provide some details on this unit's work, for its investigative objectives differ from those of other police units. First, as ICTs are constantly evolving, the team's investigators regularly receive training so that they can keep up with technological changes and the ever-inventive methods of operation of cybercriminals. Second, given that the nature of the documents inspected may be upsetting, the investigators are followed by a psychologist so that they have an opportunity to vent their perceptions of content that can be very difficult to view. As Perez and colleagues (2010) point out, police officers who work in these types of units experience direct victimization and suffer from poor psychological well-being. The more officers are exposed to indecent content, the higher the level of secondary traumatic stress disorder and cynicism. Both people in the field and experts commented on the need for support. Third, the investigators are required to understand the world of children and how they use ICTs, for they are sometimes called upon to play the role of teenagers in order to infiltrate predator networks. They must also be fluent in the various chat, texting, and even sexting lingos.

Legal Issues Surrounding the Definition of Child Pornography

A number of legal difficulties may pose obstacles to police work with respect to child pornography. Specifically, there is the issue of the variety of legal definitions of child pornography. In the late 1990s and early 2000s, most Western countries passed statutes to better control the exchange of child pornography in cyberspace, but disparities among national legal codes exist, even though on November 23, 2001, twenty-three countries, including Canada, signed an international convention on cybercrime to combat exploitation of children – child pornography, child prostitution, trafficking in children, and child sex tourism.

    In other words, even though the signatories to an international treaty agreed to jointly fight child pornography in cyberspace, their respective laws diverge in many regards. The means implemented to protect children, the age of sexual consent, and the age of majority vary from one country to the next (Khan 2000; Carr 2001; Roy 2004). The age of majority ranges from seventeen to twenty-one years, depending on the country. And there are notable differences with regard to age of sexual consent; some countries, such as Mexico, have set it at twelve years, whereas others, such as India, have set it at eighteen years. Thus, a common definition of child pornography is elusive; consider, for example, that in some countries a picture of a thirteen-year-old girl is considered acceptable under the law. Nevertheless, most countries have established the age of sexual consent at between fourteen and sixteen years.

Carr (2001) nevertheless points out some common aspects among different national laws to fight child pornography. First, all agree on the idea that child pornography is composed of images, descriptions, and/or portrayals of sexual activities involving children or minors. Second, all laws take account of the variety of computer media that make this kind of content accessible. Finally, these countries emphasize the sexual nature of the portrayal of children – that is, they try to distinguish child pornography from "innocent" images, such as photographs of children taking a bath in a naturist context or pictures of an artistic nature. Of course, the definition of "artistic nature," like the concepts of "minor" and "child," is likely to vary from culture to culture.

These legislative disparities are blatant when one consults the 2006 National Center for Missing and Exploited Children report that assesses the child-pornography laws of the 184 Interpol countries in terms of the following criteria:

- The law deals specifically with child pornography.
- It provides a definition of child pornography.
- It expressly criminalizes offences assisted by computer.
- It criminalizes the possession of child pornography, independent of the intention to distribute.
- It requires Internet service providers (ISPs) to report suspected child-pornography cases to the police or another mandated organization.

Countries are evaluated on these criteria on a scale of 1 to 10, with 10 being the best score. In the view of the authors of the study, the results obtained were "disturbing," because only five countries received a perfect evaluation (10): South Africa, Australia, Belgium, France, and the United States. Twenty-two other countries, including Canada, received a score of 8 out of 10, because they did not include in their statutes an obligation for ISPs to report illicit content distributed via their networks. Finally, the authors of the report observed that as of 2003, ninety-five countries still did not have specific legislation to counter online child pornography (National Center for Missing and Exploited Children 2006).

A number of legislative changes were made to the Canadian statute following this study. First, details were added through Bill C-2, *An Act to Amend the Criminal Code (Protection of Children and Other Vulnerable Persons)*. The amendments in effect since November 2005 have, among other things, broadened the definition of child pornography by adding audio recordings and written material "whose dominant characteristic is the description, for a sexual purpose, of sexual activity with a person under the age of eighteen years."[1] It must also be noted that the above study does not take account of the efforts made to fight the wide variety of forms that distribution of child pornography might take. For instance, aside from images and videos featuring children, Canada bans written and audio child pornography. The Canadian Criminal Code also outlaws the advocating and counselling of child pornography and simulation of a sexual activity between a child and an adult. Here is an excerpt of section 163.1(1) of the Canadian Criminal Code, which defines child pornography:

> **163.1** (1) In this section, "child pornography" means
>> (*a*) a photographic, film, video or other visual representation, whether or not it was made by electronic or mechanical means,
>>> (i) that shows a person who is or is depicted as being under the age of eighteen years and is engaged in or is depicted as engaged in explicit sexual activity, or
>>> (ii) the dominant characteristic of which is the depiction, for a sexual purpose, of a sexual organ or the anal region of a person under the age of eighteen years;
>> (*b*) any written material, visual representation or audio recording that advocates or counsels sexual activity with a person under the age of eighteen years that would be an offence under this Act;
>> (*c*) any written material whose dominant characteristic is the description, for a sexual purpose, of sexual activity with a person under the age of eighteen years that would be an offence under this Act; or
>> (*d*) any audio recording that has as its dominant characteristic the description, presentation or representation, for a sexual purpose, of sexual activity with a person under the age of eighteen years that would be an offence under this Act.

Second, it is now forbidden to promote and advertise child pornography. Simply sharing or publishing a link to a child-pornography site or image is a violation. In addition, new legal provisions impose minimum sentences for a number of crimes involving sexual exploitation of children. For possession of child pornography, the minimum mandatory sentence is ninety days. Interestingly, *R. v. Landreville* presents a jurisprudential analysis by Judge Lacerte-Lamontagne,[2] in which she notes that before the advent of minimum sentences under Bill C-2, sentences ranged widely, from fines to imprisonment (Fortin and Corriveau 2013).

Third, in 2011 Canada adopted a statute that reinforces state intervention in this criminal field. The statute forces Internet service providers to report child pornography violations to the authorities. The statute provides that the ISP is obliged to conserve data on the violation, and it sets out sanctions for cases in which the violation is observed by the ISP and not reported. It should be noted that ISPs do not need to actively search for such content.

Pseudo-Photographs

Aside from the problems surrounding adoption of a universal definition of child pornography, another debate arises in the era of ICTs and concerns about the legality of synthetic images featuring children – that is, images created with editing software, which enables users to merge two images into one or to create a new image from an original one. For example, it is now possible to make photographs in which the face of a child is superimposed on the body of an adult, pubic or facial hair is deleted to make the subject look younger, an adult's breasts are reduced to make her look like a child, and so on (Skoog and Murray 1998). Taylor and Quayle (2003, 37), who have studied pseudo-photographs, have listed three main forms:

- images that are modified and sexualized through software – for example, an image of a child whose bathing suit has been removed
- separate images that have been merged into a single image – for example, the superimposition of a child's hand on an adult's penis
- a montage of different photographs, some of which are of a sexual nature.

The debate revolves around this central question: should images be banned that do not directly feature a child, but have been modified to arouse sexual excitement among child-pornography consumers, and in some cases, even nurture their fantasy world in the same way that a real image would? Some authors, such as Iacub (2010), counsel prudence regarding criminalization of synthetic images, especially with regard to legal issues surrounding freedom of expression.

In the view of other authors, even though these images do not directly feature an abused child, they must remain illegal simply because they
have been modified to create a sexual stimulus and feed the fantasy world
of child-pornography collectors just as an unaltered image would. It was
with this in mind that Canada banned the exchange and production of
pseudo-images, thus relieving investigators of the burden of proving to the
court that the images intercepted were real images of abuse.[3] Comic-book
images representing child pornography[4] are also banned in Canada (but not
in the United States). For example, Gordon Chin was arrested for having
purchased and uploaded thousands of pages containing Japanese animations
featuring adults having sexual relations with children.[5] Chin pled guilty to the
charge of possession of child pornography; he received a sentence of eighteen
months in prison, which was suspended, and one hundred hours of community service, and he was added to the register of sexual offenders for a
five-year period (Make-It-Safe 2005).

According to the Supreme Court of the United States ruling handed
down in April 2002 in *Ashcroft v. Free Speech Coalition*, which found the
Child Pornography Prevention Act unconstitutional, there are no valid reasons to ban the creation and viewing of photographs that involve children *in
appearance* and not real children (Levy 2002). In Canada, however, the laws
in force ban pseudo-photographs.

2

The Evolution of ICTs and Their Effect on Trafficking

The production and exchange of child pornography isn't new. A few years after the camera was invented, illicit images featuring children were found in the hands of private collectors, and the first arrest of a "major" collector took place in London, in 1874; the London police listed more than 130,000 photographs of children judged indecent under the law then in effect. Production and distribution of child pornography were not, however, widespread activities at the time. The images produced were artisanal, of mediocre quality, difficult for collectors to find, and very expensive (Taylor and Quayle 2003).

The growing availability of cameras in the 1960s changed the game with regard to the production of child pornography, particularly in countries where statutes outlawing this type of material were limited. In the view of Wortley and Smallbone (2006), the weak laws in a number of countries in the 1960s also facilitated the dissemination of such images. In 1977, for example, almost 250 child-pornography magazines were circulating in the United States, many of them from Europe – especially from countries, such as Denmark, where the laws were the most lax in this regard. The magazines were distributed mainly through small commercial networks that obtained their stock directly from these countries (Crewdson 1988; Tate 1990).

It wasn't until the mid-1980s that Western countries began to tighten up their child-pornography laws. Very likely, the triggering event for this legislative turnaround was the discovery, on August 27, 1984, of the corpse of a six-year-old girl, Thea Pumbroek, who had died of a cocaine overdose in a hotel in the Netherlands – the whole thing having been captured on video. Pumbroek was featured in many child-pornography videos. This widely publicized sad story brought sexual exploitation of children to the attention of governmental authorities, which began to take measures to fight against the production and distribution of child pornography in their respective jurisdictions (Taylor and Quayle 2003).

Also in the 1980s, the spread of videotape recorders facilitated the production of child pornography by making it possible to create homemade videos. The distribution of this type of material was still limited, as collectors had to take considerable risks to establish contacts with other collectors, who were just as concerned with preserving their anonymity. They thus remained isolated from one another, and the exchange networks sometimes turned out to be false networks set up by law enforcement to counter trafficking.[1] Child-pornography collectors might arrange to get together in underground sex shops, secret communities, or spontaneous meetings organized through clandestine ads in pornography magazines (Sellier 2003). Purchasing and selling child pornography beyond national borders became more and more difficult, as evidenced, for example, by the 792 seizures of child pornography made at Canadian customs between 1986 and 1992 (Gendarmerie royale du Canada 1994). In short, all of these factors – difficulties with finding other collectors, a dearth of material, and risks inherent to exchanging material – made it relatively easy for law enforcement to repress this type of illegal trafficking (Wortley and Smallbone 2006).

The Birth of Cyberspace: A Turning Point

The popularization of cyberspace in the mid-1990s completely transformed the nature of child-pornography exchanges among collectors. The expansion of the Internet and the use of information technologies by an ever-growing number of individuals facilitated the accessibility and distribution of such content. In 1995, just before the Internet boom hit the United Kingdom, Greater Manchester Police Abusive Images Unit G intercepted twelve indecent images of children in paper or video format; in 1999, the unit seized almost 40,000 computer files (J. Carr 2004). Numerous changes also occurred in how child pornography was exchanged as the Internet emerged and became popular. Among the most significant changes were the following (Wortley and Smallbone 2006):

- The absence of geographic borders in cyberspace created access to a growing number of child-pornography images from all corners of the world.

- The virtual nature of cyberspace made exchanging child pornography more anonymous, as communications on the web could be conducted using virtual identities.
- The virtual nature of cyberspace made this material intangible, making it more difficult for law enforcement to seize.
- Images could now be distributed at a low cost, often for free, among collectors.
- The images available in cyberspace were generally of good quality, easy to store, and offered in a variety of formats.
- Access to digital images made it possible to create new ones by modifying the originals (a technique commonly called morphing).

Production of Child Pornography

Despite a few divergences, countries fighting against child pornography trafficking have all adopted laws forbidding the production, distribution, and downloading (possession) of this type of material. According to most governments, adequate repression of child pornography requires attacking production of this type of material, which inevitably requires the abuse of children. Because most collectors are looking for original material, demand for new images is always increasing, thus encouraging new production. And, of course, there are the individuals who record their own assaults for personal reasons and might later make this material available to a small group of friends or distribute it on a larger scale. We will return to this in Chapter 5. It is important to note, however, that even today many of the images that circulate in cyberspace come from old magazines or videos that have been digitized. The vast majority of the material found in Usenet newsgroups analyzed by Taylor (2001) was more than fifteen years old, with a fairly large number of images produced in the 1960s and 1970s.[2]

Moreover, growing access to ICTs has meant that it is not rare today to see sexual abusers distribute images of their assaults. As mentioned above, Statistics Canada data (Kong et al. 2003), as well as data published by International Save the Children Alliance (2005) in Europe, show that year after year, almost 80 percent of sexual assaults on children are committed by a family member or friend, or by someone close to the child. These findings concur with the conclusion drawn by Rimer (2007), namely, that the majority of child-pornography producers are family members (37 percent) or known to the child (36 percent).[3]

An existing relationship between victim and aggressor is no doubt one reason that many of the children in the images are smiling: the aggressor counts on his close, even emotional, relationship with his victim. These smiles also encourage aggressors, physical or virtual, to overlook the harm that they are causing or have caused to children. One of the tactics used by cyberpedophiles surfing the Internet to seek out encounters consists of drawing on the young person's sympathy in order to gradually gain his or her trust. As bonds of friendship are woven, going so far as sharing secrets – as the adult, for example, answers the child's questions linked to his or her curiosity about sex – it is later more difficult for the child to denounce the person (or persons) who abused him or her (see Lanning 1992).

Can we then conclude that all kinds of aggressors (strangers or family members) will be incited to film their assaults, leading to an explosion of child pornography on the Internet? In other words, do the majority of these physical aggressors film or photograph their acts and, if so, how many of them distribute these images? The information gathered to date is not sufficient to enable us to answer this question. But we may imagine that these aggressors, who use various stratagems to ensure that abused children keep silent, would be unlikely to leave traces of their assaults by filming them and distributing them widely on the Internet.

To commit this kind of intimate crime, prudence and discretion are certainly necessary. Wolak, Finkelhor, and Mitchell (2005) observe that most of the images found on the computers of victims' close relatives had not been distributed. About one-third of the individuals arrested had, according to their confessions, distributed child pornography. The authors recognize that defendants deny distributing such images, in order to avoid further incriminating themselves, but nevertheless conclude that the production (and distribution) of child pornography is not yet very widespread, although there are no doubt private collections – whose number is difficult to assess – reserved for personal use (Rettinger 2000). It is also very likely that the quantity of photographs available and known to researchers and law enforcement represents just the tip of the iceberg.

Distribution: A Wide Variety of Means

The logical follow-up to the production of child pornography is distribution and transmission of this material to one or more people via the different technological means available on the Internet. Some will distribute their images on the web, whereas others will exchange them within smaller groups such as online communities (private or public) or newsgroups, or by instant messaging. As we shall see below, child-pornography collectors have adopted different Internet services a function of their needs and requirements.

Although they were originally created for conversations on different subjects in synchronous mode, chat rooms, as semi-private meeting places for collectors, constitute sites of predilection for the exchange of child pornography. Chat rooms allow users to enter into direct contact with each other for the purpose of exchanging child pornography (Forde and Patterson 1998; Fortin and Lapointe 2002). As far back as 1997, researchers of the COPINE (Combating Paedophile Information Networks in Europe) project studied chat rooms in two IRC (Internet Relay Chat) networks.[4] Researchers observed that 518 child-pornography collectors used IRC to exchange child-pornography images and to role-play, with some adults playing the role of children (Carr 2001; Wortley and Smallbone 2006). In 2004, Roy observed that IRC was the most frequently used means of exchange (69.4 percent of cases) used by people arrested by the Sûreté du Québec's technological crime squad for possession and distribution of child pornography. In New Zealand, 79 percent of defendants stated that they had used IRC to procure child pornography (A. Carr 2004).

The software used for IRC networks offers users F-serve functionalities, which resemble peer-to-peer technology: an Internet user can draw from a bank of files stored by a user of his or her choice, without the latter knowing his or her identity. F-serve simply makes a copy of the file from the supplier's computer to the requester's computer. This new way of exchanging files is very efficient, as "the software itself regulates the exchanges without the protagonists communicating directly, in the traditional sense of the term" (Berberi et al. 2003; our translation). Users can thus leave their computer on, go to work, come home, and see the new files that have been transferred to them in their absence.

Few studies have looked specifically at email as a tool for the dissemination of child pornography, although this service is part of the arsenal of means used by child-pornography consumers. In 2004, A. Carr observed that 28 percent of individuals arrested stated that they had used email to obtain illicit content. However, in our view, email is more typically used to broadcast spam emails encouraging Internet users to view and, ideally, subscribe to, child-pornography websites. That method has declined with the efficiency of spam filters. Email is used primarily to consolidate privileged relationships among collectors who trust each other, or to communicate with young people. It is thus not an essential element in the distribution of child-pornography images and videos.

Peer-to-peer (P2P) technologies enable two users to exchange files stored on their respective computers without going through a server. This technology was originally invented to allow music lovers to exchange their music collections using services such as Napster. Today, P2P networks allow Internet users to share many different types of content, such as music, photographs, videos, and software. In short, users who so wish may offer all of the files stored on their computer to another user, who agrees to reciprocate. The presence of child pornography on P2P networks was demonstrated during a search of twelve keywords related to child pornography (General Accounting Office 2003). Out of the 1,286 files obtained this way, 44 percent (543 files) contained child pornography, according to the authors. In 13 percent of the files, "child erotica" was found; the General Accounting Office defines child erotica as "sexually arousing images of children that are not considered pornographic, obscene, or offensive."[5] There is one reservation regarding the conclusions of this study, however: it seems that the classification was made on the basis of the names of the files and not by directly analyzing the content. As we shall see in Chapter 4, this method is far from infallible when it comes to determining the nature of a file, as the title may not correspond to the content. However, a more recent study on keywords associated with child pornography (Steel 2009a) shows that even the simplest terms – those that may be used by an apprentice child-pornography consumer, such as "pedo" and "preteen," or simply an age ("5 y.o." or "5 years old") – may give relevant results. The authors conclude that these keywords may be linked to other, non-sexual, searches; nevertheless, certain terms are well established in child-pornography circles. Many users can learn the pertinent keywords by analyzing search results. The example of the keyword "PTHC" (preteen hard core) leads the authors to conclude, "This indicates a level of sophistication in those searching for child pornography on peer-to-peer networks in using terminology specific to the subculture" (Steel 2009a, 563). A study of all searches made on the eDonkey P2P network in 2007 and 2009 indicates that the searches associated with child pornography are stable over time (Le Grand et al. 2010).[6] Another author observed that such searches account for about 1 percent of all searches on the Gnutella network (Steel 2009a).

According to Carr (2001) and Wortley and Smallbone (2006), numerous files containing child pornography are exchanged via P2P technologies, because police detection is unlikely, as the exchanges are made in private between two Internet users, without ever transiting through a central server. In fact, Steel (2009b) found that searches on search engines for terms associated with child pornography dropped by about 60 percent between 2004 and 2008. In Temporini's (2012) view, the most likely explanation is that media publicity around police operations encouraged child-pornography consumers to find new virtual sites. There was thus a shift towards search tools that give a sense of greater anonymity to users, such as P2P networks. However, this belief seems to be less and less connected to reality, as the police can now use automated surveillance software on these networks (see Liberatore et al. 2010). Some authors have found that the most popular resource for acquiring and distributing child-pornography photographs and videos is P2P software, such as BitTorrent and Gnutella. It also seems that these exchange networks have seen the strongest growth in recent years with regard to the number of child-pornography images trafficked. The presence of such images is evidenced by growing numbers of complaints (General Accounting Office 2003), an increase in the supply of images and of arrests related to P2P networks (Steel 2009a; Wolak, Liberatore, and Levine 2014), and searches linked to child pornography (Steel 2009b). This means of obtaining content seems to have grown considerably according to examinations of the hard disks of people arrested in recent years, rising from 4 percent in 2000, to 28 percent in 2006, and exploding to 61 percent in 2009 (Wolak, Finkelhor, and Mitchell 2012).

One study concludes that most of the content found on P2P networks is composed of files that have been widely copied and shared on other computers (Wolak, Liberatore, and Levine 2014). Collectors seeking new content must therefore learn about virtual sites beyond P2P networks, which do not offer interesting enough results. One example is a new image-sharing tool called GigaTribe, which enables users to exchange files and chat live. It seems that GigaTribe is increasingly being used to traffic illegal content. Even though tools change very quickly on the Internet, collectors will always need new forums in which to meet each other. After the first contact is made, it matters little whether they use mIRC, GigaTribe, or the latest sharing tool. From this we gather that P2P networks constitute a gateway that is easier to use than traditional means such as search engines, and that they greatly facilitate the discovery of child pornography. They also make users aware of the terminology specific to this type of content.

Usenet is among the oldest services available in cyberspace. Created in 1979, well before the Internet as we know it today took off, this computer service functioned mainly as an electronic billboard where users could ask each other questions and find answers on various subjects. Since the turn of the twenty-first century, Usenet has evolved greatly, and its infrastructure has been adapted to make it possible for users to exchange audio and image files. Newsgroups have been used to exchange child pornography, notably because it is relatively easy for people who know a bit about computers to distribute and appropriate illicit material in almost complete anonymity. In Canada, although most Internet service providers ban such newsgroups, there are ways for child-pornography collectors to register with "uncensored" service providers, which allow access to the material. In the view of most experts on the subject, it is in newsgroups that most child-pornography images and videos are exchanged (Fortin and Lapointe 2002; Quayle and Taylor 2003; Wortley and Smallbone 2006). This is also the opinion of one of the pedophiles interviewed by Tremblay (2002): "The really interesting pictures were not found in the commercial sites but in the newsgroups." That is why we have devoted Chapter 5 to this service.

Opinions diverge on the prevalence of illicit images. Some state that they are common and relatively easy to find on the web.[7] Others believe, rather, that it is unlikely that a search conducted on traditional search engines using keywords such as *child porn* or *pedo porn* will lead an Internet user directly to child pornography (Wortley and Smallbone 2006). As Taylor (2001, 20) rightly notes, although it is very easy to find child pornography in cyberspace (not specifically on the web), "you're unlikely to stumble across it." Those holding the latter position credit the vigilance of law enforcement with regard to ISPs in this regard. It may also be that denunciations by Internet users are also partly responsible for the reduction in the amount of litigious content on the virtual spaces most often visited by the general public. We will return to this question of the accessibility of child-pornography images on the web in Chapter 4.

Aside from avoiding specific keywords known to the police (see Frank, Westlake, and Bouchard 2010 for detection techniques based on keywords), webmasters get around Internet access providers' attempts to restrict child-pornography images by indexing their sites with "unexpected" keywords (such as "volleyball" or "asparagus") or simply coded ones (e.g., ch*ldp*rn). Another strategy that distributors use to get around detection consists of tucking away a compressed ("zipped") file containing child pornography in the maze of the Internet and then communicating the password in a newsletter that will enable informed collectors to find the file.

To sum up, although the web makes it possible for individuals to distribute child pornography, it is certainly not the main distribution channel. Researchers who have questioned child-pornography collectors agree that websites do not seem to offer content that they perceive as sufficiently interesting. As one of them told Tremblay (2002, 28, our translation), "For a long time the pictures were (a) really low quality, very old, and black and white (much of it Russian); (b) more important, if it didn't look convincing that everyone was really enjoying what they are doing, then it didn't interest me and wasn't worth collecting."

Online communities are essentially Internet sites offering a series of functions that make it possible to manage relations among Internet users who share common interests. Preece (2000, 10) defines an online community as "people who interact for their own needs or perform special roles; a shared purpose such as an interest, need, information exchange, or service that provides a reason for the community; policies that guide people's interactions; computer systems which support and mediate social interaction and facilitate a sense of togetherness." Following the same principles, child-pornography consumers create online communities so that members can access and share child-pornography images and receive information on other places where they can procure them. One of these groups is mentioned in Berberi et al. (2003). This egroup used the functionalities of the Yahoo! Groups service to discuss and exchange URLs and child pornography, including images of an assault on a small girl. As the authors noted, this example "best illustrates the potential for exchanges in cyberspace" (our translation). Most child-pornography online communities that pop up on well-known websites are taken offline as soon as they are detected by the Internet service provider. Thus, to prolong their lifespan, some groups use coded names or hide the child pornography in an adult-pornography site (Wortley and Smallbone 2006).

The last step in the process of exchanging child pornography is the deliberate downloading of such material, which is illegal in most countries. Although the idea of downloading may seem obvious, it is the source of certain legal complications. Some courts do not consider visiting a child-pornography website to be downloading per se, even though police officers are able to trace all of the websites consulted by an Internet user by analyzing temporary directories on his computer. Accordingly, a child-pornography collector who surfs the web to look at illicit images, but never downloads them to his computer, cannot be incriminated. It is to avoid this kind of situation that the Canadian legislature modified the Criminal Code in 2002 to ban simply accessing child-pornography sites. Section 163.1(4.1) states,

> (4.1) Every person who accesses any child pornography is guilty of
>
> (*a*) an indictable offence and is liable to imprisonment for a term of not more than five years and to a minimum punishment of imprisonment for a term of six months; or
>
> (*b*) an offence punishable on summary conviction and is liable to imprisonment for a term of not more than 18 months and to a minimum punishment of imprisonment for a term of 90 days.
>
> (4.2) For the purposes of subsection (4.1), a person accesses child pornography who knowingly causes child pornography to be viewed by, or transmitted to, himself or herself.

Child-pornography collectors therefore have an embarrassment of riches when it comes to exchanging illicit images. P2P networks, newsgroups, chat rooms, and websites facilitate the distribution and downloading of child pornography. These new sources of supply have changed things for many child-pornography collectors. First, rapid and anonymous dissemination has simplified these illicit practices. Second, it has encouraged the creation and maintenance of deviant groups that act as sorts of communities of collectors. Finally, it has reinforced some people's belief that sexual practices between an adult and a child generally take place with the consent of the child, as the images often show children's faces with smiles or neutral expressions.

When it comes to collectors more specifically, we shall see in the following chapters that even though ICTs have made the collectors' task easier, the discovery of child-pornography images nevertheless necessitates a considerable investment of time and active participation, either by surfing the Internet (Chapter 4) or by subscribing to discussion forums and other exchange sites (Chapter 5). Thus, having a good knowledge of computers and a certain familiarity with underground sites where it is possible to conduct searches are a sort of prerequisite for child-pornography collectors (Forde and Patterson 1998; Jenkins 2001; Lesce 1999). We must remember, most child pornography is harder to find in the open areas of cyberspace, such as the web (Taylor 2001; Wortley and Smallbone 2006).

3

How Much Is Out There, and Who Are the Victims?

From a quantitative point of view, the growth of information and communication technologies (ICTs) has had an undeniable impact on the number of child-pornography images available in cyberspace. The thorny question remains, however: how many child-pornography images are in circulation? Depending on the source, the range of answers is very wide indeed. In fact, three types of estimates must be distinguished: (1) those concerning the quantity of images available in cyberspace; (2) those concerning the number of images in the possession of collectors arrested by law enforcement agencies; and (3) those systematically catalogued in databases used to identify victims.

As we noted in the introduction, the first type of estimate (concerning the number of images in cyberspace) is generally unreliable, as it is technically impossible to catalogue all of the images that circulate in a universe as labile and secretive as that of online child pornography. COPINE, one of the largest research projects instituted to analyze child-pornography images, nevertheless gives some idea of the scope of the phenomenon.[1] In 2001, COPINE researchers collected more than 80,000 child-pornography images distributed solely via newsgroups over a period of six weeks (Taylor, Quayle, and Holland 2001). Their data indicate that more than 1,000 illegal images become accessible each week in newsgroups alone (Taylor, Quayle, and Holland 2001). With the rise in popularity of peer-to-peer (P2P) networks and improvements to the surveillance tools used by law enforcement, some studies have obtained more accurate estimates of the scope of the supply of child pornography. Wolak, Liberatore, and Levine (2014) have established that in a single year (2010–11) 775,941 computers from 200 countries made child pornography available on the Gnutella P2P networks. In the United States, 244,920 computers (32 percent of all computers sharing child pornography) were observed to be offering such content. To detect child-pornography files, researchers used the file signatures of 384,000 images known to be child pornography. A critical mass of images is found on the Internet. To access them, users must make requests to file-sharing services. The requests of users seeking child pornography have also been studied. Examining the requests made by users on the eDonkey P2P networks for a number of months in 2007 and 2009, the authors observed that the number of requests involving at least one keyword with a pedophilic connotation remained stable. For both periods, 0.11 percent of the requests involved a request of this type: 141,663 requests in the first period, and 117,621 requests in the second period. When one adds to the newsgroups the images available on the web and those that are put up in chat rooms, it becomes very easy to imagine the abundance of child pornography in cyberspace as a whole.

When it comes to assessments of the collections of those found guilty of possession of child pornography, a quick glance at the headlines would seem to indicate that these collectors have a very large number of images, as the media generally give impressive numbers. For instance, one can read that an individual in Victoria, British Columbia, was in possession of 362,000 images[2] and that "police found more than twenty thousand images of minors" in the possession of a repeat sex offender in Calgary.[3] Empirical studies, however, offer a more nuanced portrait of the situation.

A. Carr (2004) reports that 106 subjects arrested in New Zealand had an average of 1,447 images each. In her research on 37 subjects in Quebec, Roy (2004) observes that on average, 2,693 files were found on their computers. She notes major disparities in defendants' collections. For instance, 8 percent didn't have any images stored on their computer, 13 percent had fewer than 100 images, 18 percent had between 101 and 199 images, and 40 percent had more than 1,000 images or videos. Two of these defendants, when arrested, were in possession of 13,000 and 20,700 images, respectively, which made them major collectors in comparison to other individuals arrested by the police. The results obtained by Wolak, Finkelhor, and Mitchell (2005) in the United States show that 4 percent of defendants did not have illicit material on their computer, 37 percent had between 1 and 100 child-pornography images in their possession, 34 percent had between 101 and 999 such images, and 14 percent possessed more than 1,000.

The above data show small differences with regard to number of images found on the computers of defendants in the United States and in Quebec, with the latter generally having more. This gap may be due to the greater weight that Quebec courts place on the quantity of images gathered by collectors, especially in determination of sentences, compared to the United States, which may motivate Quebec police officers to thoroughly analyze defendants' computers. At least, this is what Wolak, Finkelhor, and Mitchell (2005) imply when they suggest that the number of images on the computers of American defendants should be adjusted upward, because the computers aren't always examined carefully, as the investment in time and money is often too high for police organizations to bear. Thus, it is likely that the data gathered by Roy (2004) are more accurate than those cited by Wolak, Finkelhor, and Mitchell (2005).

What we must retain from these statistical observations is that the majority of those arrested collect these types of images. This conclusion is also drawn by Action Innocence (2008, 27; our translation), which notes that "most pedophiles possess child pornography material," but cautions that "a link between consumption of such material and acting out has not been proven."

Access to this type of material will no doubt become even easier in years to come thanks to the constant and rapid evolution of ICTs, notably with improvements to file-compression techniques, Internet connection speeds, and information storage capacities (Fortin and Roy 2007; Sellier 2003). In fact, a police officer testified during a trial in Quebec that individuals who possess more than 5,000 photographs and videos on their computer have become the norm (Savary 2005).

Notwithstanding the actual number of images found in cyberspace, however, the overriding concern is always the number of victims and their identification. Many police organizations have acquired victim-identification programs, which are used to analyze child-pornography images in order to find new victims.[4] Organizations study all of the images in order to uncover clues, find links between images, and identify known series. For instance, the National Center for Missing and Exploited Children (NCMEC), the leader in this type of initiative, examined nearly 15 million documents to identify more than 1, 600 children.[5]

The NCMEC's Child Victim Identification Program has reviewed and analyzed more than 132 million child pornography images since it was created in 2002.[6] It is estimated that since 2003, when the image bank contained about 450,000 unique images, almost 100,000 sexually explicit images have arrived each week on the desk of the organization's director – although these are not necessarily new images, as some may have already been catalogued. Finally, it should be noted that since the *Ashcroft v. Free Speech Coalition* ruling in the United States, identification of child victims of abuse has come to be of primary importance in that country, as it is now up to prosecutors to establish that children were actually used in these images.

The Content of Images

What exactly is the nature of the images found on collectors' computers and on the Internet? As part of the COPINE project, Taylor, Holland, and Quayle (2001) formulated a classification of child-pornography images by systematically analyzing more than 80,000 images and 400 videos. The images were classified along a 10-level continuum ranging from advertising images featuring children to images of bestiality and sadism involving minors:

- The first level is called *indicative*. It involves material that is neither erotic nor sexual and comes mainly from commercial sources such as catalogues and photo albums. The children are not nude, but dressed in underwear or bathing suits.
- The second level, *nudity*, involves images or videos of partial or complete nudity in an appropriate setting (such as a photograph of a child in a bathtub).
- The third level is called *erotica* and involves surreptitiously taken photographs of children in underwear or nude.
- *Posing* is the fourth level. It involves intentionally suggestive posed pictures of children.
- The fifth level is called *erotic posing* and involves images and videos of a sexual or provocative nature.
- What distinguishes the fifth level from the sixth level, *explicit erotic posing*, is that the latter emphasizes the child's genital areas.
- The images in level seven involve *explicit sexual activity* by a child such as masturbation, oral sex, or sexual touching. However, this level involves acts performed only among children and not directly involving an adult.
- The content of images and videos in the eighth level, *assault*, involves the participation of an adult in sexual activities.

- The images in the ninth level, *gross assault,* show assaults with penetration of the child.
- The tenth level, *sadistic/bestiality,* presents images and videos with content associated with bestiality, sadism, or inflicting pain on a child.

In Australia, the advisory board on fighting child pornography has opted to simplify the COPINE typology by using only the categories of images banned under the law, or levels 6 to 10:

- images involving nudity or erotic poses without sexual activity
- images presenting sexual activities between children or sessions of masturbation by a child
- images in which there are sexual activities without penetration between a child and an adult
- images that show sexual activities with penetration between a child and an adult
- images of sadism or bestiality involving a child. (Krone 2004)

The COPINE typology gives a better idea of the wide range of child-pornography images available in cyberspace than does the Australian categorization, as it takes account of images in the lower levels (1, 2, and 3). Although they are not forbidden under the law, these images may nevertheless present a sexual interest and arouse fantasies among child-pornography consumers (Fortin and Roy 2006). This legal pornography, termed relational by Holmes and Holmes (2002), is an integral part of the collections of many child-pornography consumers who are arrested (Rettinger 2000; Tremblay 2002; Taylor and Quayle 2003).

An analysis of the material in the possession of child-pornography consumers arrested by the police shows that many of them have a modus operandi for consumption in which images in COPINE's level 1 must be understood as part of an inseparable continuum. Police investigators have observed that, in general, the images form a series in which a subject gradually reveals his or her body. The child is seen first in underwear (level 1) and then getting undressed until he or she is completely nude (level 2). Then, the child is seen in erotic poses (level 4 or 5) and eventually in sex play with another child (level 6) or an adult (level 7 or 8). In other words, the images in level 1 and 2, although legal, are an integral part of the escalating sequence of child pornography.

This inseparable continuum is somewhat analogous to child-pornography videos, which are not divided into different sequences when it is time to establish whether or not they contravene the law: the video as a whole is considered legal or illegal. In fact, it is not unusual for series of images in collections to have been made from several sequences of a single video. In other words, images should always be analyzed taking account of the series into which they fit, and not individually. The COPINE classification also facilitates the work of law enforcement agencies when the images found on a defendant's computer must be categorized as the prosecutor prepares his or her case. In Quebec, it was used in *R. v. Beaulieu.*[7]

According to COPINE estimates, between 300 and 350 children were victims of sexual violence (level 7 or higher) in the images most recently found in newsgroups (Taylor, Quayle, and Holland 2001). In the research conducted by Wolak, Finkelhor, and Mitchell (2003), most child-pornography consumers arrested had in their possession images showing nudity or semi-nudity, 80 percent of them also possessed images showing scenes of penetration or oral sex with a child, and 21 percent had child-pornography images presenting violence such as bondage, rape, or torture.

Almost 72 percent of the victims catalogued in the COPINE databank are girls, and the age group with the highest proportion is nine to twelve years, among both girls and boys. These observations differ slightly from data obtained through analysis of computers seized by law enforcement agencies. For example, of the images found in the possession of child-pornography consumers arrested in the United States, 62 percent of individuals had only images of girls, and 14 percent only of boys (Wolak, Finkelhor, and Mitchell 2005); 15 percent of the sample possessed images of both boys and girls. These proportions are about the same as those in the study by A. Carr (2004) in New Zealand, in which 60 percent of defendants had images only of girls; 18 percent, only of boys; and 19 percent, of both boys and girls. In Quebec, Roy (2004) notes that 32 percent of the thirty-seven people arrested had in their possession only images of girls and 16 percent only of boys. Surprisingly, in comparison to data in other studies on the subject, more than half (51 percent) had images of children of both sexes.

The children found in child pornography seem to be getting younger: 35 percent of the victims are under five years old, and of these, 11 percent are under two years old. According to Taylor, Quayle, and Holland (2001), the drop in the age of victims is explained in part by the fact that it is difficult (or even impossible) for very young children to talk about the assaults of which they are victims, in comparison to older children, such as adolescents. Of the 330 individuals arrested by American law enforcement agencies, Wolak, Finkelhor, and Mitchell (2005) found that 83 percent possessed images of children aged between six and twelve years; 39 percent, of children aged three to five years, and 19 percent, of children younger than three years. A recent study suggests that child-pornography consumers may have a wider range of sexual preferences or, at least, more deviant interests than do hands-on sexual offenders (Babchishin, Hanson, and Hermann 2011). Another study took an in-depth look at how collections were acquired and at the most common age category in the collection of each child-pornography collector (Fortin 2014). Results showed that the age category of six to twelve years was the most prevalent, as it was found in the collections of 67.5 percent of subjects. They also found that 12.5 percent of collectors had a preference for adults. The average age of subjects in all images in the sample was 9.96 years. Further research would likely uncover whether the collected images are related to sexual preferences or are part of a problematic sexual exploration.

Fortin (2014) observed that the average age of children in images in the collections that he studied was around ten years, and that the distribution of the ages of the children in the images of the collection followed an almost normal curve. Taking the preferential categories of collectors, Fortin established that at the low end of the curve is a very small number of participants, whose collections are composed mainly of images of children younger than five years. Then comes a larger group whose preferred age category is from six to twelve years. Finally, there is a smaller group with images of adolescent subjects. The small number of images of children younger than five years is similar to that observed in studies measuring the availability of images on the Internet (Taylor, Holland, and Quayle 2001), analyses of requests made on P2P networks (Steel 2009a), and studies of the sexual preferences of sexual abusers of children (Carlstedt et al. 2009). In addition, and in contrast to an evaluation of the age of children younger than five years, it is difficult to evaluate the age of subjects twelve to seventeen years old. For instance, because individuals reach biological development stages at different times in adolescence, one might hypothesize that a form of bias may be present, and that there is a tendency to overestimate the age of adolescents in images. As a consequence, it is possible that images that should have been in this category were classified in the "adult" category. A similar phenomenon occurs during police surveillance: child-pornography consumers are more likely to be arrested with prepubescent images (Mitchell, Wolak, and Finkelhor 2005).

Finally, in the data collected by COPINE, in the great majority of the recent images in levels 7, 8, and 9 – those presenting sexual assaults by adults against children – the victims are white, whereas in the images in levels 5 and 6 – erotic images that do not directly involve adults – the victims are more likely to be of Asian origin (Taylor 1999). Surprisingly, black children are almost completely absent from the images. In A. Carr's (2004) study, 93 percent of the people arrested had images of white children; 26 percent, of Asian children; 13 percent, of Hispanic children; and only 3 percent, of children of African origin. The researchers could not explain these disparities with regard to the ethnicity of victims.

One possible answer may be the increasingly "homemade" nature of the productions. We know that the majority (almost 80 percent) of sexual assaults against children are perpetrated by someone close to them and that most production of child pornography is private in nature (Badgley 1984; Gough 1993; Hames 1993; Howitt 1995; Rettinger 2000). Add to this the fact that many Western child-pornography consumers seem to be attracted to Asian and former Eastern Bloc countries – sex tourism seems to flourish more in these regions than in Africa – and there is a plausible hypothesis to explain the high proportion of white and Asian victims. It has also been observed that most of the recent material seized in the Netherlands and Sweden was produced by tourists who had gone to Asia. Some feel that there is a fairly direct link between production of child pornography and sex tourism (Fillieule and Montiel 1997). Although plausible, this link should not make us lose sight of the fact that more children are victims of sexual assault by people close to them than by unknown people who emerge on the web.

4

Are Search Engines Enabling?

In the opinion of many observers of cyberspace, the World Wide Web includes a large number of sites containing child pornography, and it is easy to view and download these illicit images. For example, in 2001, the BBC stated that more than 100,000 websites offered child-pornography images.[1] Two years later, in June 2003, *Le Nouvel Observateur* in turn claimed, "Hundreds of thousands of pedophilic photographs are circulating on the Internet."[2] The National Center for Missing and Exploited Children (NCMEC), an organization that works for the protection and respect of children's rights, estimates that 13 million child-pornography images and videos have been found on the web since 2002.[3] Most researchers agree that the quantity of child-pornography images available on the Internet is constantly growing, although these claims must be interpreted with caution, as there are numerous methodological limitations on obtaining reliable data,[4] and websites are not the main source of distribution of child pornography.[5]

It is nevertheless true that commercial websites displaying child pornography do exist.[6] One of the most highly publicized examples was the Landslide website, hosted in Fort Worth, Texas, and managed by Thomas and Janice Reedy. This site served as a portal and hosted other sites administered by webmasters situated in Indonesia and Russia, allowing thousands of paying subscribers around the world to access child pornography. According to Johnson (2001), Landslide Productions generated revenues to the tune of $1.4 million per month; users paid a monthly fee of US$29.95

to access the illicit images and videos. When arrests were made in 2001, the police discovered lists of Internet users containing thousands of names from 60 countries, including 2,329 names from Canada. It is worth noting, however, that out of these 2,329 people, 141, or 6 percent, were arrested for possession of child pornography (see Alexy, Burgess, and Baker 2005; Rettinger 2000; Howitt 1995).

In May 2006, Google, in turn, was accused in the United States of promoting and profiting from child pornography. According to the charges, Google was the biggest and most effective distributor of child pornography in the world.[7] Refuting these allegations, Google maintained that it banned all forms of child-pornography distribution on its pages and systematically withdrew this type of content from its index whenever it was discovered. In Google's defence, the astronomical quantity of web pages indexed by its search engine – numbering in the billions – makes it impossible to control the content completely.[8] Consultation of the databank kept by ChillingEffects.org, one of whose functions is to catalogue all requests for withdrawal of web content judged offensive, shows that Google regularly removes sites considered problematic from its search index.[9]

Child-pornography sites on the web are detected by Internet users, by law enforcement agencies, by child-protection sites – such as Cyberaide.ca in Canada and NCMEC in the United States – and by child-defence groups, such as Perverted Justice,[10] which believes itself entitled to distribute photographs and full identities of abusers or presumed abusers – a right that is open to abuse. Fortunately, this type of extreme measure, which is reminiscent of the private vengeance of Ancien Régime vigilantism, is not tolerated in Canada.

Search engines also take part in initiatives to fight child pornography. Google and NCMEC collaborated to detect abusive images on the Internet,[11] and Yahoo became involved with Child Exploitation and Online Protection, and was one of the founders of the Home Office Task Force on Child Protection and the Internet Watch Foundation, organizations working to protect young people on the Internet.[12] Of course, such initiatives enable these firms to act as good corporate citizens and avoid being accused of facilitating access to illicit content, particularly child pornography. Moreover, they cannot be accused of being completely passive regarding the situation, or of trying to profit from the child-pornography trade.

Two conclusions may be drawn from the above. First, child-pornography images are in fact available for free on the web. Second, an assessment of exactly how many are available is not practical, given the countless methodological limitations inherent to trying to count them, and the demagogy and sensationalism that too often prevail over scientific and empirical rigour. Rather than try to approximately quantify the unquantifiable, the appropriate question is: Can average users, those who use mainly traditional search engines such as Google or Yahoo to surf the web, easily obtain child pornography?[13] In other words, can the average Internet user access this type of material without trying very hard (even by mistake), or must he put some effort into his search? People accused of possession of child pornography often claim that they fell upon these sites by chance; they plead that the illegal images found on their computers are there inadvertently and they knew nothing about them. We cannot say unequivocally that it is impossible to receive child pornography by error, either via spam email or while surfing the web (notably on adult pornography sites). However, based on our research, this is more the exception than the rule. We simply want to show that such cases are unusual, and even that most child-pornography collectors, who conduct searches with the very specific objective of finding this type of illicit material using traditional search engines, have trouble reaching their objective.[14]

As one may imagine, a considerable part of the web invariably remains invisible to most Internet users. This is the Deep Web: web content that is not discoverable by standard search engines, which only indexes part of the Web, the Surface Web. Nevertheless, the best tool for assessing the overall accessibility of public sites is search engines, which are employed by Internet users throughout the world, particularly in Canada. We chose Google and Yahoo, because, according to ComScore, they were the most popular search engines in Canada. For example, in 2004, 62 percent of all searches made by Canadian Internet users were made using Google; Yahoo, Google's closest competitor, was used at least once a month by 40 percent of Internet users. We felt that it was relevant to employ two search tools since we wanted to limit as much as possible the biases inherent to search engines' indexing methods. In fact, notable differences emerged between Google and Yahoo.[15]

In our prospecting for child pornography, we selected five keyword groups, in consultation with the investigators of the Sûreté du Québec's technological crime squad. It was their expert opinion that these keyword groups constituted a representative sample of terms used by Internet users, both novice and experienced, hoping to obtain child pornography. The five keyword groups are *child porn*,[16] *pedo porn, preteen porn, lolita porn*, and *nymphets porn*. The term *child porn* is used more by neophytes conducting searches, whereas *lolita* and *nymphets* are generally used by initiates, as these terms are used in the collector community to designate child pornography. We will present our search results in increasing order of keyword specificity, according to their level of complexity and accuracy, from the most obvious terminology (*child porn*), used by beginners, to the most specific (*nymphets porn*), used mainly by more experienced Internet users. In meetings with the Sûreté du Québec investigators, we were able to establish that it is ordinarily by successive attempts that users learn to target their search terms.

In Search of Child Pornography: Data Collection

Here is how we proceeded: first, we conducted Google and Yahoo searches to obtain a list of the sites accessible for each of our keyword groups. Then, we kept the top 100 results listed for each of the five keyword groups, for a total of 1,000 sites (500 from Google and 500 from Yahoo). Of the 200 sites retained per keyword group, 20 were chosen at random for qualitative analysis. The sample for our content analysis was thus composed of 200 websites (20 sites per keyword group, per search engine). For ethical reasons and because we were interested in sites with free-of-charge access, no pay site was visited, especially because Internet users who pay to access sites that offer or link to child pornography will subsequently have difficulty pleading ignorance. In addition, if the result of the search was, for instance, "www.test.com/images," only this site was explored. Because the web is, by definition, a labyrinth of links and interrelated sites, this measure was necessary in order to avoid getting lost in the maze. Furthermore, the objective of the study was to see whether it is easy to find child-pornography images with just a few mouse clicks, and not whether such images are available on the web. Finally, and again out of concern for methodology, data collection took place in the Internet surveillance office of the Sûreté du Québec on February 10, 2006.[17]

It goes without saying that we conducted our prospecting without activating the filter against offensive content available on the search engines – which limits access to sites deemed problematic – in order to increase our chances of finding child pornography. In this regard, Yahoo is slightly different from Google, because it publishes notices to its users to make them aware of content indexed by its search engine. First, Yahoo Canada offers the option of filtering the content offered but specifies up front that the filter is not infallible. Second, Yahoo Canada emphasizes to users that it is forbidden for people younger than eighteen years of age to access explicitly adult content. Finally, Yahoo Canada offers users a direct hyperlink to the Royal Canadian Mounted Police website, which offers a guide for safe web surfing.

Google also makes it possible for users to filter the web pages that will be displayed. There are three levels of filtering. The strict filter blocks access to texts and images with content classified as adult. The moderate filter (the default filter) impedes access to pornographic images but not texts. And with no filter active, all results from a search are presented. Unlike Yahoo, which informs its users of the existence of filtering tools from the start, Google obliges users to click on the Google SafeSearch link to obtain information on how the filter works and find out that the filter cannot be 100 percent effective. In short, Internet users who wish to increase their chance of finding child (or adult) pornography will first have to deactivate these filters.

Frightening Figures

At first glance, a user who conducts a search for child pornography may be surprised by the results. For each of our five keyword groups, Google and Yahoo indexed an impressive number of sites. The search made with the expression *child porn* resulted in 7.19 million pages on Google and 11 million on Yahoo. Of all the keywords, the smallest number of sites was obtained with *nymphets porn*: 1.1 million sites on Google and 286,000 on Yahoo. These numbers are surprising, because this search refers less directly to child pornography – as noted above, Sûreté du Québec experts consider this term to be restricted to initiates. In addition, the gap in number of results obtained between the most "obvious" keyword (*child porn*) and the most "complex" (*nymphets porn*) is significant and makes plausible the hypothesis that some refinement in the terms used is required when one wants to find child pornography.

Table 1 shows the raw results obtained by keyword searches. These quantitative results, though stunning, tell us nothing about the content of these websites; they indicate only the number of links accessible via each search engine for each keyword.[18] In fact, any Internet user could tell you that the sites listed by search engines often do not provide direct access to the information sought. Thus, these raw data are not very reliable indicators for assessing the real amount of child pornography on these websites, which may in reality contain adult pornography, other types of content, or even invalid pages, rather than child pornography. An analysis of the content of

TABLE 1

Number of websites listed per keyword group, per search engine

			Keyword group			
	Child porn	Pedo porn	Preteen porn	Lolita porn	Nymphets porn	Total
Google	7,190,000	1,510,000	3,540,000	1,940,000	1,150,000	**15,330,000**
Yahoo	11,000,000	944,000	2,000,000	4,100,000	286,000	**18,330,000**

these sites is therefore necessary to make clear that it is not so easy to find this type of illicit material online (just as it is nearly impossible to obtain a representative sample because cyberspace is constantly changing and composed of billions of web pages).

What Exactly Do These Sites Contain?

Our first content analyses revealed four categories of sites. First, there were purely informative sites, listed mainly when a search was conducted with the keywords *child porn* or *pedo porn*. These are sites that fight against child pornography, and that essentially aim to inform Internet users about issues related to the use of the Internet. For instance, the Stop Child Porn and Child Exploitation site provides cyber-investigators with a guide to child security on the Internet, and proposes a panoply of resources ranging from 1-800 phone numbers to hyperlinks to sites where users can report child pornography. There are also news sites reporting current events linked to child pornography, including arrests and convictions of Internet users charged with possession, distribution, and other offences linked to cyber-pornography. Finally, there are sites on the different laws around the world governing child pornography on the Internet.

Second, there are invalid web pages – sites that are simply no longer online. Twenty of these pages were found in our sample. It must be noted that this observation holds true only for our analysis period, as many "litigious" web pages have a short lifespan. Clearly, many such sites are deactivated and put back online with a new name and URL to make their detection more difficult (Berberi et al. 2003).

Third, there are "other content" sites. These sites offer content that has nothing to do with adult or child pornography. We found them quite often in our research. In fact, it is not unusual, in a search for child pornography, to find virtual casinos, online pharmacies, and credit services. Very likely, these sites sometimes use the keywords specific to our study to attract curious Internet users or those who may be open to exploring other illicit content. Some webmasters also apparently use keywords evoking child pornography to attract a very specific clientele who like to play on the edges of the law.

Finally, there are sites with content linked directly to child and adult pornography. The vast majority of these were found through searches conducted with the expressions *preteen porn, lolita porn*, and *nymphets porn*. These sites contain non-informative content related to child pornography. Their content may be subdivided as follows, although one site may fall into several categories:

- Child pornography without images: sites in this category are characterized by the presence of hypertext links (e.g., *teens* and *preteens*), which invite Internet users to click through to other pages related to child pornography. In other words, these sites do not directly offer child-pornography images, but encourage users to visit partner sites that do display such images.
- Child pornography with images: these are illegal sites on which child-pornography images are found.
- Adult pornography with images.
- Adult pornography without images: these sites also offer hypertext links suggestive of adult pornography, such as *barely legal click here!*, but do not offer images.

The biggest category in our searches conducted with the three keywords that enabled us to obtain substantial content – *preteen porn, lolita porn*, and *nymphets porn* – was "child pornography without images." As mentioned above, the sites in this category are characterized by suggestive text and invitations to visit other web pages in which the subjects are "younger," "illegal," "preteen," have "no sexual past," and so on. This type of content was present in thirty-two sites in the sample. The sites were noteworthy for the quantity of keywords offered on their home page. For example, for a search with the keyword group *lolita porn*, the keywords *preteen* and *nymphets* were suggested in turn, indicating that these terms serve mainly to redirect Internet users to other websites. There were also fifteen other image-free sites composed of hypertext links, this time linking to adult pornography. We will return to the question of redirecting.

Some sites did in fact contain pornographic images, but these featured adults or young adults. Legal adult pornography was present on twenty-four of the sites in our sample. Surprisingly, even when searches were aimed at obtaining child pornography, the subjects were generally aged eighteen or older (three researchers independently assessed the photographs and came to this conclusion). Nevertheless, some of the adult pornography found on these sites consisted of images that were litigious, to say the least, under Canadian law – for example, depicting situations of violence. It was also on these sites that we found the largest number of image links to other sites (redirection links).

Finally, the "child pornography with images" category was the smallest in our research. This type of illegal material was found in only 10 sites among the 200 catalogued, and in very small quantities at that. A few images of teenagers between fourteen and sixteen years old were found, and two sites included girls between eleven and thirteen years old. In fact, this category consisted of websites presenting mainly adult pornography images, with the majority of models being eighteen or older. As Cronin and Davenport (2001, 38) rightly note, this is explained by the fact that adult pornography, which is completely legal, makes it possible to hide illicit material (child pornography).

Table 2 summarizes the results obtained by the two search engines for the three most specific keywords: *preteen porn, lolita porn*, and *nymphets porn*. These results show that, proportionally (5 percent) and on the basis of keywords used for this search, it is not common to obtain child pornography using the most popular search engines even when the keywords used are directly related to the search for child pornography and content filters are deactivated. Google listed only two child-pornography sites, and Yahoo listed eight. Of course, 5 percent of 13 million pages is still 650,000 web pages, which is a relatively high number of sites containing illicit material. It would be surprising, however, to see an individual searching for child pornography consult 13 million sites with a success rate of 5 percent and continue to use search engines as a preferred tool for finding this type of image.

In our view, these figures indicate that much more of this type of illicit material is exchanged in clandestine networks than via public websites. In addition, it has been established that the majority of websites found via searches on Google and Yahoo are promotional sites that refer Internet users to a myriad of hypertext links, which continually lead them towards other hypertext links, and so on.

TABLE 2

Types of content by frequency per keyword

	Preteen porn		Lolita porn		Nymphets porn		
	Google	Yahoo	Google	Yahoo	Google	Yahoo	Total*
Child pornography without images	6	4	1	4	10	7	32
Other content	7	12	7	2	2	1	31
Adult pornography with images	2	2	5	5	4	6	24
Non-valid web page	3	0	7	4	5	1	20
Adult pornography without images	3	1	0	5	0	6	15
Child pornography with images	0	1	2	3	0	4	10

* The total of these six categories exceeds the number of sites analyzed (120) with this trio of keywords, as the categories are not mutually exclusive.

Why Did We Find So Few Sites with Explicit Content?

The Role of Redirection Sites

Understanding the role played by redirections is an essential pillar of the hypothesis that individuals who possess child pornography would have obtained it not in a first-level search (such as the one we conducted), but only after a number of unsuccessful attempts. The content analysis shows that a large number of the sites in our sample existed simply to redirect Internet users to other sites; often, a site's home page has no specific content to offer except hyperlinks. In other words, these pages found following a keyword search served only to promote the supposed attractions of other partner sites. Our searches with the expression *nymphets porn* (the most specific in the study) using the Yahoo search engine led to the largest number of hyperlink pages (eighteen), none of which was listed in results of a search with the keyword *child porn* (the simplest expression), with either Yahoo or Google.

Finally, 99 of the 200 sites in the sample displayed hypertext links supposedly offering adult or child pornography to Internet users; that is, in 49.5 percent of cases, there was no direct access to real content from a first-level search, only access to redirection sites. With regard to the three keywords that led to discovery of child pornography (*preteen*, *lolita*, and *nymphets*), the result is even more convincing: Internet users were redirected in 67.5 percent of cases (81 sites out of 120).

At this stage, Internet users either click on a link that takes them directly to a site with content (quite rare, according to our data) or they are redirected to another site that also displays a series of hypertext links. Because of this, it is likely that they will continue their search by repeatedly selecting a series of hypertext links. The image of the carrot in front of the donkey seems appropriate: Internet users desperately seek *preteens,* and are endlessly offered a click to another site on which they will possibly access those *preteens.*

Of course, these Internet users may finally access a site in which child pornography is available or one that will ask them to pay to obtain images. But what is important here is to show that individuals who obtain child pornography on the Internet via traditional search engines will, as a general rule, have made the necessary effort to do so. In other words, the thesis of inadvertent access – of illicit material being found by chance in an individual's hands – seems implausible in most cases, as the judge in *R. v. Beaulieu*[19] remarked.

The Role of Affiliate Programs and Spamdexing

A brief explanation of affiliate programs and spamdexing is necessary for an understanding of why it is difficult for Internet users to directly access child pornography when they use traditional search engines. These two techniques are at the core of comprehension of the way the Internet works, particularly went it comes to the exchange and sale of pornography (adult and child). Affiliate programs are one of the oldest means for webmasters to make money on the Internet. Essentially, Webmaster A registers with a distributor of affiliated content (Webmaster B) and offers to bring in virtual traffic (potential customers) via hypertext links available on his web page. When an Internet user clicks on Webmaster B's hyperlink on Webmaster A's page, Webmaster B agrees to pay a predetermined amount of money to Webmaster A. A number of forms of remuneration may link the webmaster and the affiliate distributor, but the most popular, oldest, and probably simplest is pay-per-click.

Webmaster A's role then consists of creating the largest possible number of websites advertising the pages of his partner (Webmaster B), because each click brings in a royalty. To do this, he may try to reach Internet users using spam email that promote his website, suggesting that it contains the content they seek (in this case, child pornography). The great majority of people who receive spam email delete it immediately. However, the law of large numbers being what it is, it is possible that a tiny fraction of these

Internet users will go to the site in question out of interest or curiosity. This site, as we have seen, is actually a virtual storefront, without any real content – a web page composed of a multitude of hypertext links.

Another technique widely used by webmasters – and no doubt the most effective – to attract Internet users to their web pages consists of attempting to control results on search engines (such as Google and Yahoo). This is what often happens with adult pornography, for which between 70 and 80 percent of free sites listed are used mainly as bait to entice Internet users to click through to "premium services on other sites" (Rosoff 1999, quoted in Zook 2003, 1266) – in other words, pay sites. In fact, although most webmasters respect the rules established by search engines regarding terms for indexing their pages,[20] some use certain tricks to get around them, including spamdexing.

Spamdexing, a neologism that combines the terms *spam*, meaning unsolicited email, and *indexing*, which refers to Internet indexing, is a perfect example of a procedure aimed at deceiving search engines about the nature of a web page or site: the usual spamdexing techniques consist of, for example, loading a satellite page with lists of keywords (to attract search engine users who conduct a search using these words), and creating dozens of sites that point to each other (link farms) to improve their ranking in the search engines. The engines judge the quality of a page based on the number of links to it (see Nathenson 1998 for more details). Spamdexing has led to the creation of a huge number of web pages that contain only a series of empty links to improve their ranking, so that they will be on top of the list of sites displayed by search engines.

Furthermore, when Internet users are able to find an original site that offers some samples of content, they must generally register to become a member in order to access all of the content available. Once again, most Internet users will leave the site, but some will subscribe, and they will be supplied with the URL for a new website (invisible to search engines) on which they can finally view child-pornography images and videos. However, the owner of the "storefront site" doesn't offer the promised content, knowing very well that a child-pornography collector will not complain to the police to get a refund.

Some researchers have also proposed an innovative approach to finding and mapping child-pornography sites. The use of "crawling" and systematic indexing methods makes it possible to use networks to reveal the interconnections between different child-pornography websites (Frank, Westlake, and Bouchard 2010). Through this method for analyzing texts and images on sites, the authors note, police detection of pivot sites "would most effectively limit an individual's ability to travel through networks and access increasing amounts of child pornography." It thus constitutes an approach applied in the systematic search for sources of the supply of child pornography and offers an interesting research avenue in the fight against child pornography.

From the Web to User Groups

As we have observed, it is relatively difficult to find child pornography on the web using search engines such as Google and Yahoo, even when the keywords used refer directly to this type of material. It is often only following a number of attempts, and with effort, that Internet users manage to find a few child-pornography images or videos. We can now deduce two things: (1) it is quite rare for an Internet user to find this type of material by mistake or by chance; and (2) most of this material in cyberspace is not distributed via search engines, even though such images are found on the Surface Web (as is other objectionable material, from hate propaganda to bomb-making instructions). This is why, in our opinion, the current debate surrounding greater regulation or, at least, stricter control, of content offered by search engines with regard to child pornography should shift its focus to other services that allow for the exchange of child pornography in cyberspace. Consistent with Zook's (2003, 1265) hypothesis, our data indicate that most child pornography on the Internet does not transit via the usual search engines.

According to Berberi et al. (2003), even if illegal sites are present on the web, it is very possible that they are not recognized by search engines or that their webmasters deliberately choose to exclude them from the index, preferring to confine them to the Deep Web. Thus, neither Google nor Yahoo can help collectors find child-pornography content easily – but many fellow Internet users, who know where this type of content is exchanged, can help them. This is why, in our opinion, most child pornography is distributed via networks of contacts among Internet users, such as newsgroups, which prove to be propitious sites for illegally exchanging child pornography, as they offer collectors, previously isolated, an opportunity to meet virtually in a world with no geographic borders.

5

Are Discussion Forums a Classroom for Cyberpedophiles?

As we have noted, newsgroups and discussion forums[1] are an important part of the child-pornography trade. Experts say that the vast majority of illicit materials transits through these virtual sites, which are estimated to number between 2,800 and 5,000 (Wortley and Smallbone 2006; Sellier 2003; Taylor, Quayle, and Holland 2001; Carr 2001).[2] Even though it is impossible to come up with a precise number, there is no doubt that child-pornography newsgroups are an efficient mode of exchange for people who like this type of material.

Data gathered daily by COPINE since 1997 have shown that thousands of illegal photographs appear online in the 50 newsgroups analyzed each week. This is a considerable number, even though a single child may be used to produce many photographs. The number of new victims identified in the photographs and videos put online fluctuates from year to year. For example, in 1999, COPINE estimated that four children per month appeared in images for the first time; in 2001, there were about two new faces per month; in 2002, the number of new victims grew considerably, to almost 20 children in just six weeks of analysis (Palmer 2005, 62). Between 1999 and 2002, COPINE observed an increase of almost 300 percent in the number of children found in material displayed in newsgroups, as well as a rise in the number of children of prepubescent age in the most recent images. According to COPINE's researchers, between 300 and 350 of the children displayed within the newsgroups were obviously victims of sexual assault, to which were added 1,600 to 1,800 children photographed nude, for whom it is impossible to know if they underwent sexual abuse afterward (Quayle and Taylor 2003; Taylor, Quayle, and Holland 2001; Taylor, Holland, and Quayle 2001).

The current situation in discussion forums and newsgroups is thus worrisome. As Holt, Blevins, and Burkert (2010, 4) note, the "Internet also provides a mechanism for pedophiles to identify and talk with others through user groups, Web forums and chatrooms." More particularly, Usenet newsgroups have been studied for evidence of crimes or deviant activities. Researchers have observed, among other things, online interactions among pedophiles (Durkin and Bryant 1999), adult pornographers, and writers of pornographic stories (Harmon and Boeringer 1997). It is therefore important to understand why Usenet newsgroups are favoured for the creation of exchange networks among child-pornography collectors. What characteristics intrinsic to these networks make them vectors for circulation of a growing number of illicit images? In other words, why are newsgroups attractive to users in general, and cyberpedophiles in particular?

A short review of the origin of the Usenet network, considered one of the oldest systems of virtual exchange in the world, is enlightening. The network has existed since 1979, well before the Internet became *the* network of networks in the mid-1990s. Developed by two students at Duke University in North Carolina, Tom Truscott and Jim Ellis, Usenet enabled users to exchange quantities of information much greater than what email boxes could hold at the time (Gakenback 1998; Sohier 1998). Versions of Usenet were subsequently developed to increase the storage capacity and the number of exchanges among users. The first public edition of a Usenet newsgroup server came online in 1982 (version 2.1). Today, a user-friendly version of Usenet enables thousands of web surfers to exchange information of all sorts (images, videos, sound tracks, and so on) in a multitude of groups hosted on local servers throughout the world. Newsgroups offer users who are passionate about a particular subject an opportunity to share documents or electronic files and to converse with others. In fact, Usenet had initially been conceived to encourage text exchanges. Only gradually was the network structure adapted to allow for exchanges of larger files, such as videos and images. Even today, some servers limit users to five thousand lines of text. To circumvent the problem of limits on the quantity of information that can be exchanged – but also for practical reasons such as shortening download time – users have developed a clever way to exchange large files: segmentation. The technique consists of dividing a large file into a number of small ones (binary files), which are then reconstructed by those who download them. Every day, a myriad of servers in the Usenet network distributes boundless quantities of messages and items pertaining to a wide variety of themes. With the transmission of text messages to binary exchanges, some estimates suggest that more than eleven terabytes of data transit through the system.[3]

It should be noted that a number of major Internet service providers, such as AT&T, Verizon, and Cox, as well as universities such as Duke, where the network was invented, have dropped access to Usenet due to lack of use. Nevertheless, third-party providers still provide access to Usenet and the content that it contains.[4] The decentralization of Usenet, in which information circulates through thousands of computers via different news servers across cyberspace, makes it particularly attractive for the exchange of illicit materials.

Another attraction of newsgroups is the anonymity that they afford. In fact, it is relatively easy for careful users to hide their IP address, thus concealing their identity in the physical world and minimizing the risk of being intercepted by the police and ultimately being charged with a crime. Well-informed users can hide their true identity and place of residence using software available on the Internet. Users who visit newsgroups without ever sending files or text messages leave very few traces of their visit; subsequent detection is thus difficult – in contrast to websites, for example, which systematically retain visitor log-in records.

Virtual communications also make it possible to avoid exchanges of physical documents (hard-copy photographs, cassettes, DVDs, and so on), which are more easily identifiable by the police. In the past, child-pornography collectors had to order tangible materials (magazines or videos), and this made police officers' work easier, because they could set up false distribution networks, disguise themselves as deliverers (of the magazine or video), and then catch offenders red-handed.[5] Of course, seizures of tangible materials still occur and are trumpeted in the media. However, for the reasons mentioned above, most child-pornography collectors now use virtual exchange networks and falsify their identity to obtain and distribute this type of material, as the discussion forums allow them to interact in real time, from the safety of their homes. Police officers are thus obliged to trap cyberpedophiles by new and complex technical means that demand a considerable investment of time and money and require extensive and rapidly evolving knowledge of ICTs.

ICTs in general, and newsgroups in particular, thus facilitate the exchange of child-pornography materials by enabling collectors, previously isolated from one another, to organize large-scale international networks for the production and distribution of child pornography. Of course, networks of pedophiles existed long before the advent of the Internet (Lanning 1984; Burgess and Clark 1984; Burgess and Hartman 1987; Lanning and Burgess 1989; Tate 1992). What has changed is their scope and the international dimension of exchanges, as cyberspace has no geographic borders. Child-pornography collectors in Kingston, for example, can converse and exchange images quite easily with collectors in Texas or Belgium via ICTs.

The existence of cyberpedophilia networks has been confirmed since the explosion of ICTs in the mid-1990s. In Hanson and Scott's (1996) view, the organized or collaborative aspect of this type of illegal traffic warrants a close look at the characteristics of these networks, in order to understand the logic that governs them. However, perhaps because child-pornography collectors are perceived as people who are socially isolated and not as individuals sharing a deviant passion, few studies look specifically at the internal functioning, and nature, of the dynamics of these social networks (Holt, Blevins, and Burkert 2010). Prichard, Watters, and Spiranovic (2011, 595) concluded their study on the prevalence of child-pornography queries on peer-to-peer networks, "Internet Subculture and Pathways to the Use of Child Pornography," by noting, "There will be great merit in future research analyzing online social-psychological dynamics and subcultural attitudes to child pornography." It is comprehension of these aspects that interests us here.

In this chapter we show the plurality and complexity of the social dynamics that are formed in child-pornography newsgroups. It is our hypothesis that discussion forums and newsgroups are organized networks for the production, distribution, and consumption of child pornography within which a subculture of deviance is developed. By using the term "network," we are emphasizing that child-pornography collectors organize themselves to facilitate exchanges, institute rules to ensure that the network operates well, and share technical and security advice so that they are not recognized and intercepted by the police. As in many networks, deviant or not, it is by active participation in the group's activities that participants are appreciated, understood, and acknowledged by the other participants, and that roles are distributed within the virtual community. In short, through a process of exchange and learning from each other, users who like child pornography come to belong to a deviant subculture that supports them in their deviance, which consists of fantasizing about children.

The sociologist Howard Becker (1963) suggests that deviance can be envisaged as a complex social process in which individuals (social actors) collaborate to institute a deviant subculture and occupy a specific position in the symbolic construction of this deviance. This collaboration enables them to have a sense of sharing a behaviour that is deemed deviant by the rest of society. The concept of deviance thus refers to a label given by a dominant group or specific institution (the criminal justice system, for example) and with which an individual or group of individuals must deal. Gradually, as the deviant behaviour is shared and experienced with others, it appears legitimate in the eyes of the participants. Becker (1963, 38) states, "Members of organized deviant groups of course have one thing in common: their deviance. It gives them a sense of common fate, of being in the same boat."

Of course, a subculture in the virtual world is different in certain ways from one in the physical world, because members can create an identity that doesn't compromise them. The virtual nature of the social actors gives rise to a relatively high degree of anonymity with regard to the outside world, which certainly attenuates the fear of being discovered not only by people they know (Corriveau 2010, 384) or by the police, which may lead to being arrested, but also by members of their subculture, and this reduces the pressure that members may feel to encourage other members to remain active in the deviant group. Unlike in other deviant subcultures, such as street gangs and traditional organized crime, those with virtual identities involved in the community may leave it without fear of later being bothered by their former "colleagues" or suffering reprisals.

Beyond the characteristics that seem to distinguish the virtual deviant subculture from subcultures that bring together individuals in the physical world, the subculture that develops within child-pornography newsgroups has intrinsic aspects similar to the subculture described by Becker (1963) for marijuana smokers. First, the child-pornography subculture is created after recurring exchanges among the members, who gradually develop a variety of social relations. To join the group, newcomers must gain the trust of the community's members through a series of commitments, ranging from participation in the exchange space to sharing illicit images to learning the internal codes and rules of conduct. Second, reciprocal moral support and the sharing of technical knowledge are the elements that make up the subculture, ensure its continuation, provide protection for all involved, and optimize the quality and quantity of pictures and videos distributed to the community as a whole. Third, social recognition is important, and it is gained according to the level of involvement and the roles played in the community concerned. McAndrew (1999) has observed this division of roles (and specialization of tasks) in criminal networks (as has Becker in organized deviant groups). As he emphasizes, it is when an illicit activity involves complexity and requires various specialized skills, as is the case for child-pornography groups, that a criminal network is formed and crystallized. Finally, participants in the subculture develop a rationale that normalizes their deviant behaviours, even convincing them of the validity of their deviance. The subculture that forms around child pornography thus helps "its members resist the effects of external stigmatization while offering them a framework for legitimization through their exchanges" (Corriveau 2010, 384; our translation).

To better understand the nature and internal operations of virtual networks of child-pornography collectors, we followed three active newsgroups for a period of 45 days.[6] This stretch of time proved to be long enough to capture the complexity and diversity of social interactions created among child-pornography collectors and to obtain an overview of the scope of the distribution of child-pornography images in these groups. In under two months, more than 24,000 communications in the form of individual messages were gathered (texts and/or binary files) and classified.[7]

Much More Than a Network for Exchanging Images

According to our data, most of the exchanges among the users of these three newsgroups involved binary files (images and videos) rather than text messages. More than 85 percent of the messages were images or binary files essentially portraying children eight to sixteen years of age.[8] When a video is exchanged, however, the distributor must split it into a hundred small files to send it (the video must later be reconstructed by uploading all of the fragments to be viewed); this inevitably increases the proportion of binary files in comparison to text messages, which require only a single transmission.

Our discourse analysis of more than 1,600 text communications brought to light the importance of conversation for these child-pornography collectors and captured the diversity of social relations that develop among them.[9] In fact, the majority of participants exchanged text messages and not images: more than 80 percent (82.4 percent) wrote at least one text message, whereas 23.9 percent sent a hybrid or binary file (video or photograph). This observation has two implications. First, it suggests that most child-pornography collectors have little new pornographic material to share and that a minority of participants are relied upon to obtain and provide such material. No doubt, the majority do not have the technical expertise required to retrieve or send images or videos. According to our data, a minority of members distribute the vast majority of illicit content offered in newsgroups: in newsgroup A, four users put online 51.7 percent of all child-pornography images present in that group, and two users distributed 72 percent of all images offered in newsgroup B. In group C, fourteen individuals were responsible for sending 50.2 percent of all images and videos. These small groups of individuals may be designated "power posters." We will return to this.

Second, it seems that child-pornography collectors consider discussion forums to be privileged spaces for conversing with other like-minded people. The newsgroup is a place where they can feel accepted and understood. The discussions that we analyzed highlighted the need felt by many to emerge from their habitual isolation, belong to a community, and converse about their deviance. Messages proclaiming the importance of the virtual community in an individual's life were not uncommon. More than simply a site for exchange, newsgroups are, according to a good number of users, a place where they feel comfortable and at home. Many messages eloquently described how much users valued being part of a specific community, a "small society" on the margins of the greater society. One of them summarized the situation perfectly: "For many of us *this is our social life*. We can discuss our feelings here and feel a part of something without fear of being condemned by society for our feelings and beliefs" (emphasis in original).

The conversations that they have within the group give child-pornography collectors the sense of having a common destiny and being part of a community in which all members have the same passions and desires with regard to children. In fact, the discussion forum is often the only place where they can talk about pedophilia without too much fear of being bothered by the police or the rest of society. This is conveyed in the lasting quality of exchanges among users, which testifies to their loyalty towards, and interest in, their virtual community.

We observed that a number of users appeared to have been communicating with each other for a very long time. They could recognize each other despite the apparent anonymous nature of the exchanges. Some users know each other so well that they can detect when others use one of their members' pseudonyms. Experienced users will not hesitate to accuse a participant of being a law-enforcement officer, for example. It is as if identities, even virtual ones, retain distinctive signs that, in the eyes of their friends, are difficult to imitate. Reinforcing this idea of a tight-knit virtual community, users state that they will exchange information only with pseudonyms that they have known for a long time. For example, Pseudo 1 informs new arrivals, "From now on, I'm only replying to messages posted by nicks *I recognize as part of this community*" (emphasis in original). In other words, one must patiently pay one's dues if one wants to be fully integrated into the network. Newcomers must prove their credentials in order to be accepted into the group.

A widespread method of checking bona fides consists of asking a newcomer to exchange child pornography with the rest of the group. Performing this illegal action forces the Internet user to compromise himself and obliges police officers who try to infiltrate the group to place themselves in an awkward position, as, by law, they cannot commit this type of infraction. In light of the many precautions that users take in their interactions, they are undeniably aware of the illegality of their activities.[10] "That is regardless if it was a relation based on love or lust, law doesn't make a difference about it anyway," one of them summarizes. Another reminds a colleague that he or she is just as guilty as anybody in this group for just viewing these articles. Why are you looking in this group in the first place? Obviously you have viewed the files and know what is posted in this particular group Yes it is well known that one of our best friends has been arrested, but you know as well as the rest of us that it is illegal to view as well as post these kinds of articles. If anon feels threatened and that he can't trust anyone here, he will move on to other areas and post elsewhere." In the view of Holt, Blevins, and Burkert (2010, 8), "One of the most significant normative orders in the pedophile subculture is the relationship between pedophiles and the larger society. Forum users clearly recognized that their sexual orientations were different, causing them to face extreme social stigma in the real world."

From Mutual Assistance to Confrontation

An analysis of the discourse of users offers a convincing argument that a lively virtual community exists within these newsgroups. In addition to recognizing that they belong to a very particular subculture, the group members develop all sorts of interactions that range from assistance and moral support to conflict and opposition.

Assistance and support are the first forms of interaction that emerge from content analyses. These are vital relationships for any community, virtual or not, because they encourage solidarity among members through mutual assistance. These relations also facilitate integration of new participants, consolidate links among members, and encourage them to stay active within the community, despite the many difficulties encountered when it comes to "living one's deviance." Holt, Blevins, and Burkert (2010, 10) make a similar observation in their analyses of five web forums run by and for pedophiles, in which "individuals agreed with one another and offered a great deal of support, reinforcement, and encouragement." As Becker (1963, 39) observes for marijuana smokers, integration into an organized deviant group enables an individual to learn "how to carry on his deviant activity with a minimum of trouble. All the problems he faces in evading enforcement of the rule he is breaking have been faced before by others. Solutions have been worked out."

Mutual assistance, which ensures that the group will survive, and perpetuates the deviant subculture, is manifested first by the transfer of technical knowledge and security rules from old members to new members who have gained their trust. The exchanges centre on help and technical assistance offered mainly by initiates, who are knowledgeable about the technologies, to "newbies," run-of-the-mill users who are trying to familiarize themselves with the many difficulties inherent to ICTs. Although they aren't computer experts per se, the initiates have acquired solid expertise on many technical tricks and techniques that conceal their identity from the physical world by restricting the information that they transmit on themselves and that can be used to trace them. As a general rule, they use computers intensively, and through both trial and error and advice from experienced users they have familiarized themselves with the latest and most advanced computer-security software.

Two main forms of help and technical assistance stand out. First, there is basic advice on protection of users' physical identities. One user explained to his comrades, "The only posters who got busted were those who made incredibly stupid mistakes." He then listed examples of errors often committed by users, such as "posting original material with your entire face in it. Posting original material with personal identifiers in it ... Posting original material with location identifiers in it ... posting ANYTHING with our true IP address or ISP name showing in your headers."

It is quite common for a neophyte to ask the group as a whole about the security rules so that he won't be identified by police officers. These questions confirm that the members of the community are completely aware of the illegality of their activities and will not hesitate to help each other to ensure that they can navigate freely and safely in cyberspace. A classic response to this request is,

> You keep your IP address out of your headers by changing which news providers you use. The news server supplied by your ISP will usually include your IP address with every post. You can subscribe to a news provider that doesn't include your IP address, or you may even find a free news provider that masks that information.

Holt, Blevins, and Burkert (2010, 15) note, "The threat of legal sanctions led pedophiles to regularly discuss how to structure individual behavior on and offline through careful management of personal information and activities." For instance, participants in discussion groups will tell "one another how to protect their true identities and keep their computers secure."

Most of the pieces of security advice that we gathered were specific, educational, and useful to neophytes. For example, Pseudo 1 told Pseudo 2 exactly which software he needs in order to stay anonymous, how much it will cost, and where he can buy it without raising eyebrows. One can regularly read comments such as, "You can try a 3.95 $ U$ FOR LIFE (yes, for life) with XXX. XXX will hide your IP address, and by changing provider, you should also change your nickname because it is related to your past post."[11]

Some members asked the rest of the community to check the validity of their anonymity to ensure that they are using the technology "safely." To do this, a message like the ones below will be displayed as a "test message":

> How easy would it be to trace this message back to me given the information in this header? A court order may be able to get the info from your provider, but no one else can find out who you are from your header. I think. But we can see you are posting from a Mac.: -)

> Hello can you do me a favor look at the information that comes with this posing and let me know what you think is I invisable [sic] enough. Thanks Anon.

Another category of requests is linked to a lack of familiarity with computer tools, which keeps certain users from viewing, downloading, or sending images. Many users don't know how to share, view, or reconstruct a binary file or a video. It is not unusual to see a request such as, "Can anyone help me with viewing images slip?" The technical expert's answer may be very succinct – "Splitting the movie will make it easier" – or very elaborate:

Depending on the original post, your newsreader can sometimes combine duplicated (caused by the poster or server error) posts into what looks like one multipart post. If this is a file you are downloading, your newsreader will probably download it correctly, and not give you duplicate files.

How your newsreader presents the newsgroup downloaded header list to you, depends on its settings, and what it understands of the subject line of each header. Each different newsreader looks at the subject line differently, and can get confused by unusual entries in them, or even the order in which the information is written. A good example of this, is Invisible's newsreader's incompatibility with how yEnc files are posted by an older version of PowerPost, which creates a subject that his newsreader doesn't recognize as describing a yEnc post. Of course, there may be other difficulties as well.

Such examples of technical assistance and pooling of security advice among members are legion and consistent with Taylor's (1999) conclusion that technical assistance plays an essential role in the maintenance of social relations among users. These exchanges recurred throughout the forty-five days of our analysis period. Furthermore, and predictably, those giving technical advice enjoy high visibility within the virtual community, and gratitude towards them is easily perceptible. Messages such as "Thanks for the help Pseudo 1" and "Thanks for your technical support" are common.

This leads us to another aspect of mutual assistance in messages among users: moral support. Sometimes, a user states that he is depressed, tired of distributing child pornography, or fed up with being insulted about his difference and deviance. One group member writes, for example, that he wanted to die after being insulted by another user. A litany of messages is then sent by members of the community to boost his morale. Here are some examples:

Keep up the good work!

George, you are a beautiful person. I've seen your many posts you have written over time. I can see that you are a very caring man. I know of no one who would want you to die, except this Troll that caused you to post this. He wants everyone to die.

YOU are important to us. Many of us care about you and wish we could help you feel better. This in itself may not make you feel better, but we can hope.

Some users seem to wallow in the status of victim or in being misunderstood. We sometimes had the impression that these individuals like to attract attention by victimizing themselves. We shall return to this below, when we address various techniques for the normalization of deviance.

Other members of the community made a point of flattering the ego of specific "colleagues," by either congratulating them or encouraging them to remain active in the group. These are essentially expressions of gratitude or of admiration with regard to the messages sent by a member or for the central role that he plays within the virtual community. The most common examples resemble these ones:

> Many thanks you for your creations. You are an absolutely awesome poster. I just want to pay tribute to your creativeness here.

> You just crack me up ... I don't think you know just how big you are. Hey note that! I did test you, remember? I hope I can stay around long enough to watch you grow up. It's going to be a [sic] amazing experience for all of us!

> I like your posts and I hope you will continue to post, here or elsewhere, this kind of pictures because I like them. Thanks a lot again for sharing.

> Thanks for your constant efforts in sharing these wonderful pictures. I appreciated them fully (as well as your dedication at sharing them).

These exchanges often take place after the well-publicized arrest of a cyberpedophile "comrade," which destabilizes the group, especially distributors. Users then encourage "power posters" to continue with their distribution despite the risk that this involves.

> I ask you to reconsider your decision, if your degree of safety in posting hasn't changed. I am not currently downloading this movie, or any other movie posted here or in other groups. My only comment is, that as a long time lurker, and even longer time poster, you should complete whatever project you have started. It is patently unfair to whoever has decided to download your donation.

Another message also illustrates this situation: "Please finish your project and then go into lurking mode if you find that necessary. Many posters take a rest now and then. That is understandable and expected." Here, flattery is used to encourage a user to distribute his material. It is the request for new material that takes precedence, not some form of moral support. We also see requests that are much more direct and explicit about obtaining new material, with messages such as, "Please post it"; "PLEASE POST"; "OH MY ... YOU CAN SEND HERE NORMAL FILES ... PLEASE DO THAT"; and "Come on. Join the crowd and enjoy the pictures."

There are also general recommendations linked to security. These messages essentially consist of warning members of the community about strangers, particularly given the possible infiltration of police officers into the newsgroup:

> This site is closely monitored by Interpol! They who used their credit card for membership or "donations" can expect a visit by (or an invitation from) law enforcement officers soon. This is also true for all who took part in any activities linked to these pages through MSN or Yahoo. Don't even think about checking out this site without hiding your IP because if you do, your name will feature on "the list"!

> This message probably did not originate from the above address. It was automatically remailed by one or more anonymous mail services. You should NEVER trust ANY address on Usenet ANYWAYS: use PGP!!

> You are charting into dangerous waters, or should I say You are driving on a dangerous highway.

> It's probably an FBI agent.

> George, if Jeff tells you he can get you in touch with Homeanon, he is most likely LEA and is trying to trap you. Don't fall for it.

> Unsecure (OK, stupid) postings can help provide LEA with useful information to aid in what they do, but are not in themselves the cause of arrests.

Mutual assistance, gratitude, and flattery are not the only types of interactions that can arise – conflicts are also possible. As happens in all communities, virtual or not, mistrust, or even hate, sooner or later emerges, aimed sometimes at members of the community and other times at people who are not part of it.

From the beginning of our analysis, the existence of conflicts between users was evident. Some messages could even be called hateful. These examples, chosen at random, speak for themselves:

> What a fool ass hypocrite. Too complicated for U????

> All you fucking deserve is a bullet in your empty head. I understand you have become quite the big shop in the little boy diddler groups.

Wrong group Asshole!

Lookin, Has anyone ever told you how much of a fucking retard you are!!?? PLONK!!!!! Kill file time!!

Go fuck yourself, Y-Nut. Not everyone who fucking trolls your little child abuser groups is me.

What is it with you assholes in here. You know what is posted in this group and therefore if you have a problem with it, don't download.

Occasionally, these insults come from participants who are not members of the community (commonly called trolls). They denounce one of the group's members or pedophilia. One might speculate about these users' motives, as they must put a great deal of effort into getting into these illicit sites – which are difficult for the average user to access – simply to vilify the participants. Nevertheless, the trolls' opinion of cyberpedophiles is in no doubt, as the examples below show:

If you choose to post any more illegal material in this group, YOU will be reported. You then can join your friend homeanon for the next thirty years. You have been warned.

Just what the world needs. Another fucking pedo.

Spoken like a true pedo. In that case, I hate you.

From this moment forth, anyone who posts ANY illegal photos or video's of children will pay the price. I will forward ALL info to the cyber tip line and let the proper authorities deal with the poster of such illegal material as they see fit. This group has been warned.

Another, less violent form of conflict consists of making moralizing statements instead of direct insults. A child-pornography collector may express his disagreement or disgust with certain pedophilic acts, such as sexually assaulting a child under five years of age. For instance, one user openly attacks another:

Homeanon is a truly sick individual! Apart from being a childrapist, he's a pathetic liar and a hypocrite. Why? Because he turns out to be a religious maniac as well! Anyway, this message was not to me, but i feel to answer because i care about the kids also, believe it or not, but i do.

Another user simply says,

Serious, it took me years but I found out that there is no boy that enjoys sex with an adult man. They do it for goodies. That can be money, that can be a kind of father role, can be going to cinema, can be escape from bad parents. But in inner they hate sex in that age. So people are in that group and say I love boys and do that not fully platonic are liars!!!

Disturbingly, many child-pornography collectors seem to forget, deliberately or not, that all new material produced has resulted, almost always, from the physical or psychological abuse of a child.[12] It was common for cyberpedophiles to state that one must never have sexual relations with children and that members should limit themselves to looking at photographs! This type of moral reasoning also appears within discussion groups studied by Holt, Blevins, and Burkert (2010, 14), who observe, "The consensus seemed to be that 'child rape' [not consensual child love] is bad, but possessing child pornography is not bad." Some participants go further, opining, "Individuals who caused serious harm to children should receive harsh punishments," even though they state that "punishments given to pedophiles were unjust and largely because of unfounded concerns over the harm they may cause."

Finally, trickery is also part of conflictual relations among users. One might steal another's virtual identity, for example, to tarnish his reputation. Here are some examples that shed light on this practice:

Of course, we can come to trust certain posters to be truthful, but there is always the possibility of impersonation. It's happened. There are only two people in these newsgroups who can duplicate my post's headers.

I impersonated Y-Not not too long ago, over a short period of time, in several newsgroups. Everyone I know got a real kick out of it and thought I captured the essence of his personality to a tee.

ya think Anthrax & WWW are the same person ??? I think 123, Anthrax & WWW are the same flea.

It is essential to understand the importance that these users attach to their virtual identity. Indeed, although participants in child-pornography

newsgroups seek, for obvious reasons, to remain anonymous in the eyes
of society in general (and particularly of the police), they nevertheless seek
the recognition of others. Some users don't hesitate to write to the group
as a whole with the barely concealed goal of receiving compliments and reminding other members of their importance to the group. Others prefer to
act modestly to attract the recognition of other participants: "This does not
mean that I'm a know-it-all, and that I'm trying to boost the ego that isn't in
play here? There are a great many things that I know very little about."

Users, particularly power posters, want to trumpet the prestige associated
with their pseudonym. These users want to be known and recognized by all
members, and they use various means. A revealing example is that of a former newsgroup member who returned to the group specifically to re-establish
the facts related to his identity. Inactive in the group in question, he nevertheless kept an eye on his virtual reputation: "The only reason I came back
is because I heard that a few of you retards were accusing someone else of
being me. You don't have a fucking clue as to how usenet and servers work."
Another user wanted to ensure that the members of the community were
crediting him with distribution of certain photographs and set out to clarify
the situation: "You can tell the difference between me and an impostor, because I post from a Macintosh with a Mac program called XXX, and I usually
post through Newscene. I just added something extra to the header, in a way
that he can't duplicate, so people will more easily see that I use a Mac."

Some pseudonyms are also known and recognized simultaneously in several groups. Other users consider them to be the "godfathers" of the virtual
community. As Jordan and Taylor (1998) noted in their research on hacker
communities, usurping someone else's pseudonym is a practice frowned upon
by most users; it is also not recommended to change one's pseudonym, since
knowledge (and recognition) of this pseudonym allows trust to be established
among different virtual identities. The following is a good example of this.

> The trouble with nic stealing is that historically it has been used by the
> troll pros with more dubious intentions than yours. The results are im-
> mediate. Long standing friendships are tested, and some very important
> concepts such as faith and trust are ravaged. I wish at this point I could
> smoke a purple bud and sit back and follow the trail of all the ramifica-
> tions of losing things like faith and trust in everyone about everything but I
> don't have a bud to smoke. So in this moment where I can only scratch the
> surface of higher thinking, I'll have to leave it at saying it would be an ugly
> world indeed. Another way of looking at it would be to consider if this had

happened to you. Someone using your nic represents you in a way that causes those of whom you trust and like to no longer trust and like you back. Of course this is more easily accomplished on the usenet than in real life but it can happen in real life. I think it's called ugly rumors in real life. Another primitive type behavior that nic stealing evokes is the terrible feeling of ... there, but for the grace of God, go I. Your fun would have been more fun if within your impersonation posts you included the appropriate caveat.

In short, since Internet users are most interested in having their virtual identity recognized, it is apparently rare for a single individual to use a number of pseudonyms to send messages.[13] Following this logic, we noted a certain form of informal competition within newsgroups, with members seeking prestige and a social status that their peers would envy. We will return to this.

Among all the messages that we analyzed, slightly more than one third were of limited value for the comprehension of the social interactions that are formed in a newsgroup. For example, there were illegible messages – messages with no text or obvious information, such as "???" and "%%$" – and messages composed solely of onomatopoeias (such as "ohhh" and "pffff"). Other messages were coded or composed solely of hyperlinks. As mentioned above, these hypertext links are meant essentially to redirect users to for-pay websites; when one clicks on them, the associated supplier is obliged to pay a royalty to the creator of the web page containing the hyperlink. Even clandestine newsgroups can't escape spam!

We also noted the presence of opinion posts on various subjects unrelated to the issue of child pornography. These messages generally have a philosophic bent and are about subjects as diverse as the meaning of life, the principle of freedom, and the internal dynamics of newsgroups. Here are two excerpts: "One day I too will die and all of you will. The question is will you leave your mark on the world"; "We should not put people on too high a pedestal. One false step, and our feet will have company." These types of messages are not specific to child-pornography collectors, but are found in all newsgroups.

Shared Roles, and the Associated Prestige

In light of what we observed in exchanges among users, it is undeniable that roles are shared in child pornography discussion forums and that the prestige of certain pseudonyms rises as a function of the respective members' roles and involvement in the vitality of the virtual community. Roles (and the associated recognition) are shared essentially according to three criteria: the degree of involvement (active or not), the type of involvement (production, distribution, discussion, and so on), and the level of knowledge of ICTs in general and newsgroups in particular. Application of these criteria reveals five types of members in the virtual community, and these types can be placed on a prestige continuum based on the degree of recognition obtained from the other members. The internal structure of discussion groups is not strictly hierarchical, especially with regard to subordinate relationships, which are difficult to maintain in a virtual universe. Rather, newsgroups are spaces of mutual assistance and learning among members, in which social relationships are more cooperative than hierarchical.

The most-recognized participants are those who distribute (and, ideally, produce) materials – those who we have identified as power posters. They can be divided into two categories: the producers-distributors of new materials, who obviously have access to children, and the distributors, who share their collections accumulated over the years with the community but do not make new images or videos. As we noted at the beginning of this chapter, our quantitative data show that power posters are in the minority: a small number of users distribute most of the images and videos to the rest of the group. This is why they are so respected, acknowledged, and consulted by the other members. As a rule, power posters also have all the technical knowledge required to enhance their value to the group and ensure its security. This is also true for the third type of participants, technical advisors, who help to keep the group going with the technical assistance and the security advice that they dispense to average users.

Average users are the fourth type of participant in this deviant subculture. Our data indicate that they are probably the majority; they play a very important role in the maintenance and reproduction of the virtual community, even though their participation is negligible in terms of the exchange of child-pornography materials. They contribute to the energy of the group through their many interactions and their desire to be recognized by their comrades one day. Some take active part in the group's discussions, whereas others intervene only occasionally to inquire about a very specific technical problem that concerns them – for example, inability to download or reconstitute a message transmitted in fragments. Sometimes, they simply ask for a specific photograph or video to complete a collection that they like so that they can offer it to another newsgroup.

The fifth and final type of users are voyeurs, who surf newsgroups to profit from the images offered but never take part in the discussions or

TABLE 3

Participants in discussion forums by type of involvement, degree of involvement and visibility, and level of knowledge

Type	Main type of participation	Average level of participation and visibility	Average level of technical knowledge
Power poster	Production and distribution	Very high	High
	Distribution only	Very high	High (but generally lower than producer)
Technical adviser	Technical and security advice	Variable, but generally very high	High
Average user	Essentially text exchanges (sometimes images)	– Low distribution – Low to high communication	Very variable, but often limited
Lurker	Navigation	Invisible	Unknown

exchanges. These users, known as lurkers, are, so to speak, invisible both to other members of the group and to law enforcement agencies and researchers. They form the hidden face of this virtual world, and it is impossible to form even an estimate of their numbers. Thus, although they are present in newsgroups, they are not active members of the deviant subculture that is formed there.

Table 3 summarizes the types of participants discussed above. However, it is important to remember, and is worth repeating, that it is impossible to determine the prevalence of these types of participants. We cannot know whether active users are the visible minority or represent almost all cyberpedophiles. On the other hand, given our data, it seems fair to state that power posters are the minority compared to average users, who have little experience in terms of technological knowledge and skill.

The Rationalization and Normalization of Deviance by Cyberpedophiles

A final element seems crucial in the institution of a deviant subculture: justification of the deviant behaviour, so that participants are encouraged to continue their involvement in the virtual community. It is, in effect, by interiorizing positive reinforcement that child-pornography collectors manage to rationalize their deviant behaviour: "At an extreme, they develop a complicated historical, legal, and psychological justification for their deviant activity" (Becker 1963, 38). Child-pornography collectors advance various types of arguments to legitimize their actions and minimize any sense of guilt that they might develop. This capacity for legitimization and rationalization has been a constant among pedophiles, both in the past and today (see Mayer 1985; Abel, Becker, and Cunningham-Rathner 1984). A number of sociologists interested in deviance, including Sykes and Matza (1957), Scott and Lyman (1968), and Friedman (1974), have highlighted the processes that individuals use to neutralize and suspend, at least temporarily, their sense of guilt with regard to social norms that they are transgressing, while legitimizing their conduct that is disapproved of by the rest of society.

For child-pornography collectors, the first self-justification technique consists of denying any form of responsibility for their behaviour. This is conveyed by the constant use of excuses through which the individual projects the fault for his acts onto external or internal factors that are beyond his control.[14] For example, some cyberpedophiles will say that they are unable to control their sexual impulses, which are so strong that they are unable to avoid succumbing to temptation. "BoyLove is a natural thing, like being born gay or even straight. It's something you can't control or choose," summarizes one of the forum users studied by Holt, Blevins, and Burkert (2010, 10). Another form of excuse consists simply of denying the disapproved-of behaviour. For instance, an individual arrested in possession of child pornography maintains that he received these images by error via email or was spammed. In short, he has nothing to do with it, but is a victim of circumstances.[15] This is why we have made a point of debunking the theory of the accessibility of child pornography by traditional search engines. As we have shown, it is rare to obtain this type of illicit image by error (particularly when a large number of illicit files are involved).

The second technique is denying that damage is caused to the victim. Child-pornography collectors state that they have not committed real abuse to children because they simply look at images and videos. One collector states, for instance, "Please consider, there is a difference between fantasy and action," and comments, "The Master taught me; don't judge." Users regularly make statements such as, "Loving a child is not wrong or immoral and certainly should not be illegal" (Holt, Blevins, and Burkert 2010, 10). Yet, as we have noted, they forget that children have to have been abused in the physical world to produce these images and videos. Some see the children's smiles as proof that they do not come to any harm. "It seems unlikely that he was hurting the boys since no one had a clue about it. To them, it was probably just fun," said one of them; another said that he hoped that the person who took the photographs "didn't hurt these boys. I hope they truly enjoyed it."[16]

At the same time, they don't hesitate to state that the children were consenting, and that they were later grateful for having undergone such experiences. Children's right to sexual freedom is sometimes invoked: if these children are victims, they are victims of a social system that keeps them from fully enjoying a sexual apprenticeship that might be offered by loving, experienced people. In other words, it is claimed that these children, far from being victims, actually benefit from, and are made happy by, these relations with an adult. In certain respects, these arguments resemble those of the North American Man/Boy Love Association in the United States, which sees relations between consenting adults and adolescents as unproblematic because, as their website claims, a majority of young people have a positive experience through these relations.[17] Using this justification, that is, highlighting the supposedly beneficial aspects of the acts committed, pedophiles deny that their behaviour is reprehensible. Among the classic arguments are that intergenerational relations are often enriching for young people because the love that they receive helps their emotional and sexual development, and that this type of (loving) relationship entirely respects the rights of children, notably the right to experience their sexuality as they wish. As one member of the newsgroups we studied claims, "I am a lover of boys who has devoted his life to boys and has initiated them to Christ's love." Here, certain socially acceptable rules (not having sexual relations with a child) are replaced by other rules that are more just in their eyes (respecting the right of children to have sexual relations).

A third justification technique is one in which the deviant accuses his accuser – that is, a hypocritical society that hypersexualizes children and youths in advertising campaigns. In this case, child-pornography collectors see themselves as scapegoats for a society that eroticizes children even as it paradoxically becomes more and more moralizing with regard to sexuality in general and children's sexuality in particular. In our research, this was conveyed mainly by aggressive comments:

Also that the fascist pigs and various LEA's [law-enforcement agencies] don't harm the kids, If it was, and will be, that makes me very sad.

They [trolls] ascribe to us all their own ignoble qualities and motivations, because they are unable to conceive of anything that they don't have inside themselves. Trolls are unable to like others, because they don't like themselves. They *must* think of others as being beneath them, or they will be forced to see how personally worthless they themselves are. Can we blame them for that, being who they are? Have you seen any of them with a useful sense of humor? What Trolls hate and fear the most, is LOVE.

I hope they truly enjoyed what transpired and I hope the shrinks they are sent to don't traumatize them by brainwashing them with shame.

A final common justification technique consists of emphasizing that for a very long time societies and notable men have been child-pornography collectors and lovers of children (referring here to the etymology of the word "pedophile"). This technique is called BIRGing, which is short for "basking in the reflected glory of related others."[18] "Here, history is invoked to show that pedophilia has not always been so repressed, that it is not all that bad, and love of children – which is what they claim they do – must be distinguished from the assault of children" (Corriveau 2010, 396; our translation), but they brush off the fact that they themselves profit greatly from abuse of children by viewing their collected images and videos. Among pedophiles attracted to young boys, it is not rare to see references to Greek society, the cradle of modern democracy, whose renowned philosophers, including Plato and Socrates, accepted pederasty.[19] Some point out cultures in which healthy "loving" relationships between adults and youths are permitted, others that many Western societies long encouraged marriage between girls twelve or thirteen years old and adults who were twenty-five or thirty – as was once the case in Quebec, for example (Corriveau 2010, 396).

To sum up, cyberpedophiles try by various means to legitimize or, at least, excuse their illicit behaviours. In this regard, ICTs act as facilitators because they allow for mutual recognition among child-pornography collectors previously isolated from one another. Through their numerous interactions within the deviant subculture, they are more easily able to justify their deviant behaviours, for they realize that they are far from being the only ones living with this passion that is "shameful" to the rest of society. And, "Whatever the level of participation in such a 'community,' the process of obtaining photographs through the Internet validates and legitimizes such activity and provides a sense of support to those with a sexual interest in children" (Taylor, Quayle, and Holland 2001, 9; see also Holt, Blevins, and Burkert 2010; Merdian, Wilson, and Boer 2009; O'Halloran and Quayle 2010). As Prichard, Watters, and Spiranovic (2011, 588) observe, "It is worth noting here that online group norms – pro- or anti-social – are considered to be influential in terms of individual behavior (Demetriou and Silke 2003), although reference to Thornberry (1987) would suggest that this possibly depends on the degree of attachment between an individual and the group."

***

As our analysis shows, child-pornography Usenet newsgroups do in fact constitute deviant communities in which child-pornography collectors are found, have exchanges, and develop specific social relationships. Whether it is through exchange of child-pornography materials, moral support, or technical help, mutual assistance and collaboration imbue these cyberspace meeting places. The most experienced users don't hesitate to show neophytes the way, by telling them how to protect themselves from the police, how to participate more actively in the exchange of new material, and how to preserve their anonymity in the physical world without sacrificing recognition in the virtual community. These individuals, however, remain aware of the risks that they run, of their marginality, and of the illegality of their actions. This is why mutual assistance, both moral and technical, is essential to keeping the group alive.

We have also emphasized the importance that users give to their virtual identity. Users are very concerned with maintaining the reputation of their pseudonyms, notably to preserve the recognition and respect of peers who they receive within the group.

Our analysis shows, finally, that child-pornography discussion forums are composed of increasingly interdependent users, who depend on the respective skills and knowledge of each participant. Whereas one user will be venerated for the images that he publishes, another will be admired for his technical knowledge regarding the secure use of cyberspace, leading to a certain kind of specialization in the execution of tasks. Of course, this specialization is not formal and rigorous, as it is in traditional organized crime, but it is nonetheless perceptible.

6

Who Are Cyberpedophiles, and Is There a Link between Viewing and Abuse?

Trying to describe the typical profile or profiles of child-pornography collectors is not an easy task, because it is impossible to obtain a representative sample; the only individuals known are those arrested by the police. In other words, many cyberpedophiles are able to evade law enforcement. These invisible collectors represent the hidden face of the issue, and it is difficult to draw definitive conclusions about them. Some authors even posit that the suspects who are apprehended are the least adept, since they have not managed to escape the police net, and that the big players probably continue to work with impunity (Fortin and Roy 2006). The conversations in newsgroups analyzed in Chapter 5 seem to confirm this hypothesis: power posters are generally very aware of police techniques and know which new technologies to use in order to remain anonymous and undetected. Some interesting research has tried to establish sociodemographic profiles (age, occupation, ethnic origin, and other factors) of the collectors who are arrested by the police, and they have proved very relevant. In this chapter, we will give an overview of the studies that attempt to describe the child-pornography consumer. We will try to uncover common traits among the different groups of pornography collectors studied in research produced in Quebec, Canada, and elsewhere in the world. Finally, we will address the delicate question of the link between collecting child pornography (having a sexual interest in children) and acting out with abuse.

Child-Pornography Collectors in Quebec

In 2006, Fortin and Roy sketched out a portrait of all Quebec child-pornography collectors who had been charged by the police between 1998 and 2004. Using police reports, the authors categorized 199 offenders by such factors as sex, age, occupation, previous arrests, and prior criminal charges at the time of arraignment.

What conclusions can be drawn from these data? First, almost all of the 199 Quebec cyberpedophiles arrested were men: 96.5 percent of the sample, or 192 individuals. These data, as we will see below, concur with those in other Canadian and international studies. In addition, they concur with data on sexual offences, which, according to the Uniform Crime Respecting Incident-Based Survey of 2002, state that 97 percent of criminal counts of sexual offences in Canada involved men.[1] It must also be taken into account that in the seven cases in Fortin and Roy's (2006) study that involved women, six also involved a man. Deeming these to be exceptional cases, the authors did not take account of women in the development of their typology.

Second, the age of male offenders varies considerably, from 10 years to almost 65 years. The traditional image of the paunchy, moustachioed "dirty old man" is thus obsolete and erroneous. On the one hand, the average age of Quebec subjects in Fortin and Roy's (2006) study is 35.4 years; this corresponds roughly to the data gathered by Statistics Canada (Kong et al. 2003) concerning the average age of sexual offenders in Canada, which is 33 years. On the other hand, 13.6 percent of individuals arrested for possession of child pornography were younger than 18 years old when they were arrested.

As a corollary, it is not surprising to find a large number of students among Quebec cyberpedophiles – almost 20 percent of Fortin and Roy's (2007) sample. Being a student also proves to be the most common occupation among Quebec subjects, followed by the category "Unemployed/welfare/on disability pay," at 16.8 percent of the sample. Does this mean that idleness is the mother of all evils? At any rate, it is clear that the search for child-pornography material requires a considerable investment of time and effort.

Another characteristic worth noting is related to the criminal records of Quebec subjects: 65 percent of them had no criminal record before their arrest. This proportion is even higher in Roy's (2004) study, in which 86.5 percent of individuals in the sample had no criminal record. Fortin and Roy

(2007, 480) also note that only 10.4 percent of defendants had previous arrests for crimes of a sexual nature.

Four Typical Portraits of Quebec Child-Pornography Collectors

Although it is not possible to paint a typical portrait of child-pornography collectors, for the methodological reasons given above, Fortin and Roy (2006) were able to establish a typology of Quebeckers arrested by the police for possession of child pornography, through taxonomic analysis of the sociodemographic data, specifically, the subjects' criminal history. The factors used to construct this typology are age, number of previous arrests, the sexual nature of these previous arrests (possession of child pornography and other crimes of a sexual nature), and whether or not the subject was a student.

From this analysis, four typical portraits emerged (Fortin and Roy 2007). The first, and most common, is the *explorer*. These individuals are twenty-four years old on average, typically students, and have no criminal record. According to Fortin and Roy (2006), the explorer is usually a young man who "just wanted to see what it was" but who, paradoxically, proves to be an assiduous collector. The case of François is typical. Revealed to the Quebec authorities by the German police and arrested soon after having distributed child-pornography images on the Internet, François – twenty-one years old, single, a computer sciences student with no previous arrests – justified his behaviour to the police this way: "I didn't take any personal photographs, and I didn't make these photographs available with the goal of causing harm to anyone." Aware that it is illegal to hold and exchange this type of image, François nevertheless had in his possession no fewer than eight hundred child-pornography images and videos featuring both boys and girls (Fortin and Lapointe 2002). Similarly, Ludovic, twenty years old, also without a criminal record, explained to the police that he had simply been curious. An in-depth analysis of his hard disk brought to light more than ten thousand photographic and audiovisual files of child pornography, which were there unbeknownst to his girlfriend (Fortin and Lapointe 2002).

The second typical portrait is that of the *solitary pervert*. Almost fifty years old (forty-nine years on average), this individual acts alone; as he interacts little with the child-pornography-collector community, he essentially finds his images and videos on commercial sites or by responding to offers of illicit content on the Internet. The solitary pervert has the financial means to pay for the material that he wants to obtain via credit card. He also has only a slender criminal dossier. For instance, a twenty-nine-year-old man was arrested as part of an international police operation for having visited a child pornography pay site. Pornographic images of boys were found on his computer (Fortin and Roy 2006).

Very similar to the solitary pervert in terms of average age (late forties) and criminal record, the third typical portrait is that of the *organized pervert*. He is distinguished by his active involvement in virtual communities such as those described in Chapter 5. Through his numerous interactions with peers, he is able to enhance his collection of images and videos featuring children. For instance, Serge, thirty-nine years old and in a common-law relationship, was arrested by the police as he was making requests on the IRC network. In the search of his residence, the police found 1,500 images of boys and observed that he had been found guilty of sexual abuse and gross indecency in the past.

Even more representative is the case of Stéphane, administrator of the "Les pornographes masqués" [the masked pornographers] electronic billboard, used as a meeting place to consult child-pornography material. Collectors in this network are also known for their use of very sophisticated computer programs to distribute child pornography. The group was known, nationally and internationally, for its production and distribution of child pornography. Stéphane's role in this group consisted of posting the new material, or material found on the Internet, for redistribution to the other members. He was caught by the police because he was listed in the email address book of one of the group's members arrested some time before (Fortin and Roy 2006).

The last typical portrait, the *polymorph*, is clearly distinguished from the other three by his relatively extensive criminal history. Although there were few of them in our sample (eight), the individuals in this group, essentially men in their early forties (average: forty-two years), had a number of previous arrests, notably for sexual assault. On average, they had previously been charged with three counts of a sexual nature and had seventeen other counts when they were arrested. The investigators of the Sûreté du Québec's technological crime squad estimate that virtual abusers are the most likely to act out, as consumption of images does not completely satisfy them.

This was the case for Chris, forty-one years old, arrested for sexually touching his new wife's daughter. When he was arrested, the police officers seized all of his computer equipment: hard disks, CD-ROMs, and diskettes full of child pornography. After analyzing the images discovered in his home, the police uncovered unpublished content that seems to have been taken with the digital camera used to take family pictures. Chris defended himself by saying that the girl had invented the story, even though nude photographs of her were found on his computer. The investigators also found among the files a photograph of a seven-year-old female neighbour to whom he claimed he was giving "Internet lessons." And this was not the first time that he had had run-ins with the justice system, notably for gross indecency (Fortin and Roy 2006).

Finally, it should be noted that all of the individuals arrested in Quebec for possession of child pornography claimed personal (and not commercial) motives, which throws doubt on the assertion that the child-pornography business is organized by criminal networks eager for financial gains. Despite an increase in commercial sites, many based in eastern Europe, in recent years, observers estimate that the for-profit trade has dropped since the advent of the Internet in favour of free-of-charge exchanges.[2]

Child-Pornography Collectors in Canada and Abroad

Does the sociodemographic profile of Quebec child-pornography collectors correspond to that of child-pornography collectors arrested elsewhere in Canada and abroad? In certain respects, yes. All of the studies conducted among individuals arrested for possession of child pornography underline the predominance of men in this type of activity, with women being a very rare exception to the rule. For instance, the study by Seto and Eke (2005) conducted in Ontario revealed only one woman, co-accused with a man, in the 201 files analyzed. A. Carr's (2004) research in New Zealand also found only one case involving a woman among the 106 individuals arrested,[3] and in the United States, less than 1 percent of the sample of 429 subjects studied by Wolak, Finkelhor, and Mitchell (2005) were women. Similarly, McLaughlin (2000) found two women among two hundred subjects from forty states in the United States and twelve other countries. In addition, almost all of those convicted in Canada and the United States were white (Fortin and Roy 2006; Wortley and Smallbone 2006; Wolak, Finkelhor, and Mitchell 2005).

With regard to the average age of defendants (35.4 years in Quebec), the data are relatively similar: 35 years in Seto and Eke's (2005) study; 38.2 years in McLaughlin's (2000) study;[4] and 30 years in A. Carr's (2004)[5] studies.[6] In general, researchers estimate that the average child-pornography collector is a white man in his twenties or thirties (see Wortley and Smallbone 2006;

Wolak, Finkelhor, and Mitchell 2005; Strano 2003). In a study comparing two samples from 2000 and 2006, the group aged eighteen to twenty-five years increased in size significantly, from 11 percent to 18 percent, from the first period to the second one (Wolak, Finkelhor, and Mitchell 2011).

It is more difficult to estimate the number of people under eighteen years of age involved in these types of dossiers, given that police forces do not use a uniform classification, particularly when minors are concerned. Seto and Eke (2005) note, for example, that most young sexual abusers (between twelve and seventeen years old) are not in the register of Ontario sexual offenders; only those convicted as adults are included in the data. Fortin and Roy (2006) in Quebec (13.6 percent), A. Carr (2004) in New Zealand (14.15 percent),[7] and McLaughlin (2000) (10.5 percent) nevertheless inventoried slightly more than 10 percent of defendants of minor age. This proportion was only 3 percent in Wolak, Finkelhor, and Mitchell's (2005) sample in the United States.

Wortley and Smallbone (2006), like Wolak, Finkelhor, and Mitchell (2005), found that child-pornography collectors are generally college-educated workers,[8] and noted in passing that judges, teachers, dentists, police officers, and other professionals have been arrested for this type of crime. This wide variety of professions thus makes untenable any attempt to build a typical employment profile of defendants.

Studies diverge more with regard to whether the profile of those accused of possession of child pornography includes having a criminal record. In Quebec, 10 percent of defendants had a criminal record related to sexual abuse at the time of their arrest (Fortin and Roy 2006). In Ontario, Seto and Eke (2005) estimate this proportion to be 31 percent;[9] for New Zealand, A. Carr (2004) assesses it at 11.3 percent. Recent studies suggest that online offenders have a significantly lower criminal history than do contact offenders against children (McWhaw 2011). Although it has been observed that Internet-only child-pornography offenders present major socio-affective problems, they have low scores on criminal lifestyle, antisocial cognition, and criminal behaviours and attitudes scales (Magaletta et al. 2014).

In light of the above, it seems quite ill advised to attempt to "set" the sociodemographic profile of the child-pornography collector. First, the subjects analyzed (persons charged) do not form a representative sample of child-pornography collectors; they are only the ones who are visible and known to researchers. In fact, they are merely the ones who got caught by law enforcement agencies, and constitute only a fraction of all criminals.

TABLE 4

Age of persons arrested

	In Quebec	In the United States	In New Zealand
18–25 years	20.6%	11%	17.3% (20–24)
26–39 years	31.7%	41%	30.8% (25–39)
40 years and over	37.2%	45%	18.9% (40+)
Total number	192	429	185

Note: We did not include the study by Seto and Eke (2005), because these researchers do not include the ages of the defendants.

Second, the characteristics analyzed differ from researcher to researcher, making any attempt at generalization difficult. Nevertheless, in the view of Strano (2003), the "average child pornography collector," if he exists, is a single man aged between twenty and forty years, without a criminal record and socially integrated, with an average to high level of education and an intellectual-type job (student, liberal profession, and so on) (Action Innocence 2008).

What is important to bear in mind is that child-pornography collectors do not form a homogeneous group: they are men, but of all ages and all vocations. Depending on the study, they may be ten to seventy years of age; belong to any social class; be unemployed, students, or blue- or white-collar workers; and have a high-school diploma or a university degree.[10]

Evolution of a Sociodemographic Profile

The data presented above allow us to compare those charged with possession of child pornography today with those charged before the advent of the Internet. In Burgess and Clark's (1984) study of child-pornography collectors in the United States, undertaken several years before the explosion of the Internet, 90 percent of the collectors were aged thirty years and over, with an average age of forty-five years. The vast majority of the fifty-five subjects studied belonged to the upper-middle class, and 34.6 percent of them had a criminal record for sexual offences. However, in the above-mentioned studies, the average age of people charged is now about thirty-five years and the proportion of those older than thirty never rises above 65 percent. In addition, twenty-first-century child-pornography collectors come from all social classes, with a large proportion composed of unemployed people, students, and blue-collar workers. Finally, individuals with a criminal record for sexual offences are much less numerous in the samples in contemporary research than in those by Burgess and Clark (1984) (10 percent, 11 percent, and 24 percent, versus 34.5 percent). Wortley and Smallbone (2006) observe that the proportion of individuals with a criminal record arrested for possession of child pornography has dropped since the advent of the Internet from between 20 percent and 33 percent to about 10 percent today (see also Dobson 2003; Wellard 2001; Smallbone and Wortley 2000). One could thus hypothesize that the popularization of ICTs has meant that experienced old-school pedophiles are now lost in a sea of the curious newbies. This would explain, in part, why there are proportionally fewer abusers in most of the studies.

However, major methodological limitations do not enable us to test our hypothesis. Because they favour anonymity, both in exchanges of images and in production of such images for personal purposes, ICTs minimize the chances of a collector being arrested and thus having a criminal record linked to this type of offence. It is indeed much easier to use a digital camera to make images than a traditional camera, which necessitates the use of a darkroom, money for photographs, and storage space to preserve them (Lööf 2005). Because digital cameras are easy to use and make it possible to store a large quantity of material in a single computer, they favour the creation of personal images in the comfort of the home; at the same time, they reduce the risk that collectors leave traces of their activities and thus be detected by law enforcement agencies.

The Need to Collect: What Child-Pornography Collectors Have in Common

Another change with the advent of ICTs has been the growing accessibility of illicit materials. Previously, collectors had to be highly motivated, resourceful, and, often, ready to spend substantial amounts of money to find and obtain child pornography (underground magazines, photographs, video-cassettes – often a copy of a copy of a copy). Today, the child-pornography market has no borders, is open to all, and is generally free. Of course, some collectors are still faced with technical constraints. However, as we have shown in Chapter 5, Internet users may quickly find networks that can help them overcome these difficulties.

A common trait among collectors, both of yesterday (before the advent of the Internet) and of today, is worth noting: most of them feel the need to constantly collect more images and videos. As Quayle and Taylor (2003) have noted, many collectors are not satisfied with the number of acquisitions that they have in hand. This is the main reason that a large quantity of child pornography is usually found in defendants' computers; it is not unusual to find more than a thousand photographs.

Muensterberger (1994) states that the central aspect of collecting is constant possession of the object prized by the individual. The collector is captivated by the effort that he must make to overcome the obstacles that separate him from the acquisition of a new piece (Taylor and Quayle 2003). Although collectors are distinguished from each other by the objects that they choose to collect, these individuals have some points in common. First, the object of their collecting must be accessible, and the articles that compose the collection must be classified and arranged. Second, the individual devotes much time and money to collecting, and this brings him great pleasure (End Child Prostitution and Trafficking 2002).

Many studies have examined the fundamental role that collecting plays in the lives of child-pornography collectors (Lanning 1992; Tate 1992; Klain, Davies, and Hicks 2001; Quayle and Taylor 2003; see also Armagh, Battaglia, and Lanning 1999). Most collectors are constantly trying to increase their collection, which they always see as too small. Collecting becomes an integral part of their life. They almost never destroy anything (and this is appreciated by law enforcement agencies, because it usually means a successful prosecution). They carefully choose the photographs that will supplement their collection. And they feel intense pleasure when they are able to complete a series of images on a particular theme. Images that are difficult to obtain become "hunting trophies." The need to possess new images incites many to participate actively in various exchange networks. Increased visibility in newsgroups, however, increases the risk of being found out by the police who monitor these forums.

Researchers emphasize the variety of functions that collecting fulfils for child-pornography collectors. In this regard, cyberpedophiles are not really different from their predecessors, who did not have access to the virtual world to enhance their collection. The Internet, ICTs, and computers only encourage collectors and facilitate their "desire-need" to organize, classify, and, especially, expand their collection (see Lanning 1984; Burgess and Hartman 1987; Tate 1992; Wyre 1992; Hames 1993; Muensterberger 1994; Howitt 1995; Belk 1995; Gaspar and Bibby 1996; Levesque 1999).

First of all, collecting allows collectors to obtain sexual gratification – to experience their sexuality through the sexual fantasies that this type of illicit material elicits for them. Second, collecting fulfils a number of other functions. Our investigation of the social interactions in newsgroups in fact convinced us of the immense gratification that a collection provides to its owner. "Good collectors," who have varied and rare collections, quickly gain the esteem of their comrades, and, as a consequence, prestige and envy within the virtual communities in which they interact. As we showed in Chapter 5, users' quest for recognition for their pseudonym is at the very core of the dynamics of these newsgroups. In fact, as Taylor and Quayle (2003) have suggested, the collection also acts as currency among collectors. A collector may use his collection, for example, as a means to negotiate the acquisition of new images that will enhance his collection; at the same time, he acquires a certain form of social recognition from his peers.

The possession of child-pornography images, like the social relationships woven within newsgroups that we discussed in Chapter 5, are also used to reinforce collectors' belief in the validity of their pedophilic "passion." The images confirm that they are not alone in the world, that other people share their passion and they are not so deviant after all. Obviously, the development and democratization of the Internet have facilitated the creation of online communities that allow deviants of all sorts to "discuss their problems in a sympathetic and non-censorious environment that may be lacking in their everyday lives" (Ferreday 2003, 284). In the view of a number of authors, the virtual context allows child-pornography collectors and pedophiles to find each other (Holt, Blevins, and Burkert 2010; Prichard, Watters, and Spiranovic 2011). Collecting activities thus contribute to the consolidation of their deviance.

For the collector who abuses, the images have one more use: they are the sword of Damocles hanging over the head of their victims, whom they can blackmail (see Lanning 1992). Children are made to understand the risks they run if they denounce their abuser. They are told, for example, that the photographs in which they appear will be revealed to their friends, parents, or relatives, causing irreparable harm to them and those close to them. For some of these young people, who were active in the initial encounter with an individual whom they knew was an adult and whom they trusted, the feeling of guilt may be very strong.

For some, of course, these images may encourage escalation to sexual assault, or be used to sexually disinhibit young people: "If others have done it and liked it [their smiles in the images being the proof]," they say to their victims, "why don't you give it a try?"

It should be recalled that one favourite tactic of cyberpedophiles is to gain the trust of the young people whom they target, notably by establishing friendship, sharing confidences with them, and taking the time to answer their many questions about sexuality. Then comes a form of psychological manipulation aiming to make the young people feel guilty if they denounce the abuser, by reminding them of the role that they play in the relationship. As one of the reports by Action Innocence (2008, 6, our translation) notes, many cyberpedophiles "have been able to exploit the emotional vulnerability of adolescents, either by responding to the distress that they are experiencing in the search for their sexuality, or by manipulating them psychologically." Clearly, the report emphasizes, the abusers "have drawn the sympathy and gradually gained the trust of their victims by establishing an emotional or confidence-based relationship."

Finally, there is an underlying function for a small subgroup of consumers who act out: images represent the sum total of their hunt for, capture of, and conquest of victims, and this enables them to maintain connections with people and experiences that no longer exist. Without the collection, the author's act and accomplishment may be forgotten (Warren, Dietz, and Hazelwood 2013).

Categories of Child-Pornography Collectors

From these different functions of collecting, authors have developed typologies of child-pornography collectors on the Internet, which show a number of similarities with the categories formulated before the advent of the Internet. Below, we will analyze these studies. But first, we would like to present a short summary of attempts to categorize the collectors of child-pornography images. As far back as 1984, Hartman, Burgess, and Lanning painted four profiles of child-pornography collectors, which are still relevant today. First is the collector who secretly keeps his images, the *closet collector*. In general, he has obtained the images from commercial sources in order to avoid entering into contact with other individuals. At the same time, this person rarely abuses children in order to increase his collection, especially because he is aware of the harm that abusing children causes. His collection enables him to have his sexual fantasies without acting out.

In this sense, the closet collector is different from the *isolated collector*, who doesn't hesitate to use his personal collection to desensitize and groom his future victims. Then there is the *cottage collector*, who seeks to share his collection in order to legitimize his deviance as much as possible. Finally, there is the *commercial collector*, who sells and exchanges his images. Some commercial collectors have no personal interest in child-pornography images. What they want is to make money via this illicit commerce (Fontana-Rosa 2001).

Klain, Davies, and Hicks (2001) broadened and refined this typology, by integrating into it these individuals' levels of organization and participation in the collectors' community. For instance, the *trader* was distinguished from the cottage collector. Whereas the latter abuses children and shares his collection with peers, the former communicates frequently with other collectors but does not commit sexual abuse.

A continuum of child-pornography collectors is thus apparent, ranging from those who simply view the material in private to those who abuse, produce, and sell child pornography on a small or large scale.[11] In general, at the lowest risk level is found the simple *collector*, who takes no violent action other than possession of illicit material. At the second level is the *traveller*, who is more interested in meeting youths than in increasing his collection. To do this, he manages to worm his way into chat rooms where he is likely to come into contact with young people. To facilitate an eventual encounter with a young person, he uses different subterfuges, including luring, for which he takes on a fictional teenage identity. At the top level is the *producer*, who is constantly looking for new victims in order to increase his collection, and then uses this new material as currency to further enhance his collection (Fortin and Roy 2007; Rettinger 2000; Howitt 1995; Badgley 1984).

In his sample of 200 individuals arrested for possession of child pornography, McLaughlin (2000) estimated that there was one producer per eighteen collectors. It must be noted that, in spite of various media reports, the great majority of producers do not charge for their product, and they thus have no monetary interest in it. As mentioned above, the thesis that the child-pornography trade is controlled by organized crime has not been proven. On the contrary, a 2002 report by End Child Prostitution and Trafficking emphasizes that since the advent of the Internet, the distribution and production for commercial purposes have plummeted, and private collections have become more and more numerous. This is also what our empirical data indicate.

An Italian study divided cyberpedophiles into four categories, according to the risk that they will commit assaults (Strano 2003, cited in Action Innocence 2008, 29). First, there are *voyeurs* – child-pornography collectors who do not have physical contact with children and are simply trying to find new material. They represent 89 percent of the individuals arrested by the police. Then, there are "combination" cyberpedophiles, who are divided into two categories: first, those who essentially collect images and assault children from time to time; second, those who regularly look for new child pornography but also frequently assault children. These people represent, respectively, 8 percent and 2 percent of the individuals arrested by law enforcement agencies. Finally, there are pedophiles whose behaviours are focused on sexual abuse and who are able to meet young people through the Internet. They use the images that they collect mainly for arousal or as sexual substitutes.

Krone (2004) has formulated a nine-level continuum of risk for child-pornography collectors, based on their investment in the search for child-pornography, their degree of involvement in collectors' networks, their technical capacity to protect their real identity, and the nature of child abuse that they may commit (viewing versus sexual contact). The first typical portrait is that of the *browser*, the Internet user who accidentally (e.g., through spam) discovers child pornography, but who deliberately preserves it on his computer. He is practically undetectable by the police, as he does not actively search for illicit images. The situation is the same for the *private fantasizer*, who creates his own virtual (digital) child-pornography images or texts.

Krone (2004) then distinguishes three types of collectors who more actively search for illicit materials: the *trawler*, the *non-secure collector*, and the *secure collector*. What differentiates these three types is their level of knowledge of the security rules that protect anonymity, and their awareness of the degree of risk involved in acquiring new material. The trawler mainly browses the web in search of child pornography or child-pornography networks, without being too aware of the risks that he incurs. The non-secure collector, also not very aware of the risks, searches for new material in discussion forums. The secure collector searches only in closed, often secret, networks, and uses encryption software when he exchanges photographs of children. He understands very well the risks inherent to his desire to collect child pornography, and that is why he exchanges his collection only in secure networks. Like the four preceding types, he does not try to actually abuse children, as his collection enables him to experience his deviancy at the level of pure fantasy.

Before going further, it is of interest to examine the question of the use of technologies, as reported in recent Quebec studies. The recent data show that it is generally the collectors who are less technically adept and less well equipped who are caught by law enforcement agencies (Fortin and Roy 2006). For instance, 65 percent of people arrested had what was termed as basic equipment, and fewer than 10 percent had in-depth knowledge of computers; furthermore, 71 percent of them did not use passwords to protect their information. This proportion grows to 77 percent when it comes to the use of encryption software and to 81 percent when it comes to software that cloaks users' identities (Wolak, Finkelhor, and Mitchell 2005).

In the case of the next three types described by Krone (2004), sexual abuse is added to possession of child pornography. The first level is the *groomer*.[12] This Internet user uses ICTs (the web, P2P, discussion forums, etc.) to establish contact with young people, either by passing for a teenager or by using child-pornography images to disinhibit young people and encourage them to perform sexual acts, either in his presence or remotely via webcam. Sometimes he exchanges his new discoveries with peers; sometimes he keeps them for his personal use. His exposure to risk depends largely on his capacity to keep his victim quiet or to recognize police officers posing as potential victims in discussion forums.

The groomer generally uses the following technique or modus operandi. First he tries to come into contact with a potential victim on the Internet, usually in chat rooms. Either he poses as a young person or he targets a child who seems to have particular problems (with, for example, his or her parents, or with exploring his or her sexuality) and counts on his "authority" and adult experience to establish a relationship with him or her. Once the relationship is established, he proposes to the young person to continue the conversation in a private chat room. This is when he can gradually establish a relationship of trust with the young person.

Grooming is also practised by the *physical abuser*, who differs from the groomer in that he has less interest in child pornography. His main objective is physical sexual abuse. If he has images of his assaults, he keeps them for his personal use. The eighth type is the *producer*, the child-pornography collector who makes images of his assaults available to the largest number of collectors possible: his prestige and recognition by peers are closely linked to the quality and quantity of images that he produces and offers to the other cyberpedophiles with whom he is in contact, especially in newsgroups. He thus differs from the *distributor*, the ninth type, who is interested only in exchanges, for commercial purposes or not, of old or new material that he has obtained through previous exchanges. He is also generally very active in newsgroups and discussion forums.

A Synthesis of Child-Pornography Collector Types

The above studies, although different in their scope and sample size, present certain similarities that should be pointed out. First is the recurrence of the diehard collector, the Internet user who minimizes his contacts with other cyberpedophiles and keeps his collection for his personal use. He is not involved in incidents of sexual abuse or assault. Different authors call him collector, voyeur, explorer, chatter, and browser.

Second is the marked presence of the collector-distributor, who is generally characterized by his degree of involvement in child-pornography-collector communities and level of technical knowledge of ICTs. These two factors influence researchers' categorization. Thus, depending on the study, he is called the cottage collector, the secure or non-secure collector, or the solitary or organized pervert.

Finally, found in all of the studies is the collector-abuser, who has committed sexual abuse and is distinguished by the frequency of his abuses (traveller-producer or temporary, frequent abuse), modus operandi (physical abuser, seducer, producer, polymorph), and use of images of abuse (isolated collector, in-house collector, and commercial collector). In fact, many researchers underline the importance of the producer/trader. He frequently combines the functions of production (abuser), distribution, and, of course, possession (collector) for personal, or sometimes income-producing, purposes (the income-producing aspect is not well documented).

However, all of these studies look at people who have been investigated and arrested by law enforcement. Thus, in our view, one type of child-pornography consumer remains in the shadows: the one who likes these images but doesn't collect them. He is a viewer – he looks at images but never downloads them. Sometimes he browses pay websites; other times, he finds images in newsgroups or elsewhere in cyberspace. However, the proportion of these people among cyberpedophiles is probably quite low, given the important role of compulsion in the search for content on the Internet. It is also very possible that cyberpedophiles, who have devoted great effort to finding the images that they desire, hope to preserve them in order to eventually use them as currency – especially because, thanks to ICTs, storage capacities are now considerable.

The figure below summarizes the different profiles presented in the research.

FIGURE 6.1 Synthesis of typologies of child-pornography collectors and abusers as a function of their actions, their level of virtual interaction, and their technical level

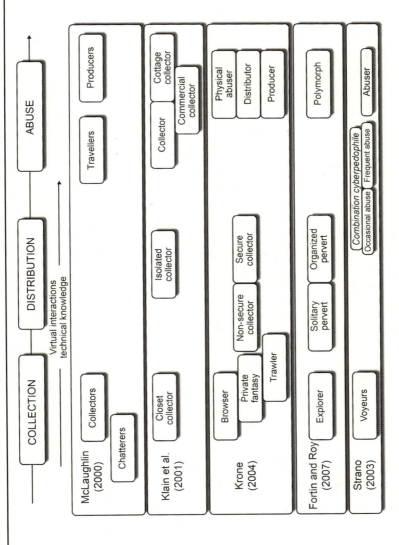

The Link between Viewing and Abuse

In dealing with child pornography in cyberspace, the researcher is obliged to investigate the effects of consumption of child pornography on the possibility of acting out by collectors. This thorny issue is worth examining, as there is no consensus among researchers on the role of child pornography as an initiating factor in acting out. In the view of some, consumption of pornography may be cathartic, because it enables individuals to inhibit their sexual impulses through fantasy, whereas others see it as an instigator, because it makes acting out – that is, abuse or assault – seem unexceptional and legitimate.

For instance, Kelly (1992) concludes that pornography predisposes some men to commit sexual abuse. In other words, viewing sexual assaults tends to trivialize them so much that it legitimizes acting out. More recently, Schell et al. (2007) concluded that at least 80 percent of individuals who obtain child pornography actively abuse children, and Bourke and Hernandez (2009) found that 85 percent of 155 people convicted of possession and distribution of this type of material had abused children. In Bourke and Hernandez's opinion, the number of child abusers hiding behind the labels of "collectors" or "consumers" must not be underestimated. In other words, a number of studies disregard the real number of abuse cases, by referring only to police statistics on the crime of possession and distribution.

In contrast, Langevin et al. (1988) compared a sample of 200 sexual delinquents with a control group of 150 individuals and found that consumption of pornography does not seem to be a decisive factor in sexual abuse. Quayle and Taylor (2003) found that only a small number of child-pornography collectors use this type of image as a prelude to sexual abuse, as most collectors limit themselves to acquiring, classifying, and viewing such illicit images. The result of a study conducted in Ontario by Seto and Eke (2005, 208) also debunks the idea that there is a cause-and-effect link between viewing pornography and sexual abuse. In fact, 75 percent of the 201 subjects in that study who possessed child pornography had no known antecedent of illicit sexual contact. In Seto and Eke's view, the data show that that not all child-pornography collectors are inclined to commit a sexual assault on children. In Sweden, the National Swedish Council for Crime Prevention estimated that between 1993 and 2003, almost 40 percent of those found guilty of possession of child pornography had also been accused of sexual assault against children (Åström 2004). Action Innocence (2008, 27; our translation), an anti-cyberpredation organization, summarizes the issue by noting, "Studies that have examined the link between sexual abuse and pornography tend overall to produce weak or inconsistent results, and thus have not been able to establish a cause-and-effect relationship."

Another argument was provided by Wolak, Finkelhor, and Mitchell: if viewing child pornography triggers and validates sexual abuse that would otherwise be suppressed or controlled, then, as availability has increased, we should see an increase in abuse in the United States (Wolak, Finkelhor, and Mitchell 2011). On the contrary, however, child sexual abuse decreased from 1992 to 2007, according to a number of sources. The authors remain cautious in interpreting these figures, stating that we cannot conclude that dissemination of child pornography has had no impact.

The debate therefore remains open, but we must not lose sight of the fact that the vast majority of sexual assaults are committed by people known to the child, and not by unknown people who hide out in cyberspace. According to the National Clearinghouse on Family Violence report *Child Sexual Abuse* (2006), in confirmed cases of sexual abuse, the vast majority of alleged abusers (93 percent) were family members or others related to the child. AuCoin (2005, 7) notes that almost 86 percent of victims of sexual assaults know their attacker: "Half of victims under the age of 6 were sexually assaulted by a family member while this was the case for 44% of victims aged 6 to 10." Of cases reported to the police, only 5 percent of victims did not know their attacker, "and of these assaults the majority of the victims were older teens aged 14 to 17 (50%) or aged 11 to 13 (24%)." Concerning more specifically the direct role of ICTs in the possible risk of assault by strangers, Loughlin and Taylor-Butts (2009, 7) note that in 2006 and 2007, there were 464 incidents of luring of children under eighteen years of age reported in Canada: "This figure represents an average of about 3 incidents of child luring per 100,000 youth under the age of 18, reported to police per year. While more than 6 in 10 child luring incidents reported to police during 2006 and 2007 were not cleared, charges were laid or recommended against an accused in about 3 in 10 incidents; the remaining offences (8%) were cleared otherwise."

Thus, a definite link between consumption of child pornography and sexual assaults against children remains to be established. A well-known case in Ontario might indicate that there is such a link: the murderer of Holly Jones, Michael Brière, admitted that he had acted out after viewing child pornography. Middleton, Beech, and Mandeville-Norden (2005) rightly conclude, however, that the viewing of adult pornography and child pornography may, *for certain individuals,* be a source of sexual stimulation that, *under certain circumstances*, also act to normalize sexually deviant behaviours and encourage the commission of a physical assault. Furthermore, the acting-out dynamic may vary from one individual or circumstance to another.

The risk level thus varies, depending on the profile of individual child-pornography collectors, including how obsessed they are with collecting new images. Whereas some are exclusively collectors, others see sexual assault as a way to expand their collection, as viewing child-pornography images incites them to produce more and more and, at the same time, legitimizes sexual abuse. In other words, either collecting is the collector's main motivation, or it is the byproduct of a desire to assault. Taylor and Quayle (2003) conclude that the main clues to predicting (to the extent possible) physical assaults by child-pornography collectors are:

- whether they possess recent images and not old images that have been digitized
- whether they catalogue them meticulously by theme
- whether they participate actively in a cyberpedophilia community
- whether they exchange images in order to expand their collection and their prestige within the community of collectors.

Fortin and Roy (2006, 124; our translation) note, "Among consumers of child pornography, only a small number commit assaults, but these people seem to be relatively active and to assault a number of victims." This observation corresponds in some ways to Taylor, Quayle, and Holland's (2001, 9) conclusion that "the process of obtaining photographs through the Internet validates and legitimizes such activity and provides a sense of support to those with a sexual interest in children." According to one study (Wolak, Finkelhor, and Mitchell 2011), for every six cases that started with possession or distribution of child pornography there is one case of sexual abuse.

This is why the effect of child pornography on pedophilic desire must be distinguished from its effect on pedophilic practice – that is, sexual abuse of children. Some collectors will experience their pedophilic desire through images; others will physically experience their impulse by acting out. What is more, the diagnosis of pedophilia is difficult to make beyond all doubt because the expert must demonstrate clinically, through either self-reports or plethysmographic data, that the individual has recurring sexual fantasies featuring prepubescent children (with an age difference of at least five years between victim and aggressor). Thus, many incestuous relatives do not meet the criteria for pedophilia, even if they have assaulted their children. Studies on this subject indicate, in fact, that 40 to 50 percent of sexual abusers of children are not pedophiles (Seto 2008, 2009).

Consequently, we do not know (and do not have the means to know) whether child-pornography collectors will sexually abuse or have already sexually abused the children seen in the images that they collect and exchange. What we do know, however, as a result of our observations, is that images of children (real or virtual) seem to encourage many collectors to want to obtain new ones, and that this indiscriminate demand results in the fact that behind these images is a child who has, in real life, been assaulted or lured or used for sexual purposes in one way or another. In addition, we must pay attention to Iacub's opinions in *De la pornographie en Amérique* (2010) on the criminalization of fantasies and the issues surrounding freedom of expression. In our view, these collectors are abusers in a virtual world, and not solely cyber-voyeurs. We have thus taken the position that the very act of consuming child pornography should be a criminal offence; our argument is that exchanges among Internet users are real in the sense that they have effects in the physical world, because children sooner or later suffer real abuse to satisfy the demand for child pornography. In this sense, we prefer to speak of the *physical world* (rather than the *real world*) as opposed to the virtual world, as we have observed that for most Internet users, the exchanges and social relations that they forge in cyberspace are in fact real, despite their inherently virtual nature. These collectors are also well aware of the unlawfulness of their actions.

Conclusion

The development of the Internet and of information and communication technologies (ICTs) has had the effect of democratizing the production, distribution, and possession of child-pornography images and videos. Whereas the acquisition of such material was once difficult, risky, and costly, it has become easy, anonymous, and cheap or even free. The virtual nature of cyberspace also offers collectors a sense of security. Armed with a simple digital camera, anyone can produce pictures and, if he wishes, distribute them to people who share his pleasure in viewing and collecting them. For child-pornography consumers who might feel remorse about their deviant impulses, the Internet also offers the opportunity to join newsgroups in which peers provide support and comfort.

The popularization of ICTs has thus multiplied the opportunities for child-pornography collectors to meet, notably by eliminating geographic boundaries. Like other researchers (see Holt, Blevins, and Burkert 2010; Fortin 2014), we have observed the effects of virtual sociability on how collectors of child pornography perceive their illicit behaviours. For example, our study reveals both the influence of pro-pedophile forums on the number of exchanges of illicit material and the effects of participation in these networks on collectors' cognition and technical knowledge. Virtual forums also provide an excellent opportunity to learn about this type of offending – a sort of crime school for child-pornography collectors. What is more, in peer-to-peer networks collectors are able to rationalize their impulses by openly discussing their attraction to children. Virtual sociability, the impacts of which are very real, also produces a certain form of social hierarchy within these networks – a hierarchy based mainly on the level of participation and the degree of involvement in the (re)production of the deviant subculture.

It therefore seems obvious that any approach to evaluation or therapy must take account of the participants' level of virtual sociability. For example, a psychosocial worker may want to discuss with the child-pornography consumer his level of involvement in forums or discussion groups in order to understand what kind of collector or consumer he is, especially as it has been shown that contact with peers makes it possible to obtain rarer and more explicit content (Fortin 2014). This type of information will help workers evaluate and treat simple collectors, who are generally solitary, differently from distributors, who necessarily have more contacts with the deviant community – with the consequent risks of acting out in the embodied world. What is more, participants in these virtual exchange and communication networks have developed technical and computer-related knowledge so that they are better equipped to outsmart the police and obtain more sought-after content.

It is essential to look closely at the characteristics of collectors in order to grasp the role that consumption of child pornography and active participation in virtual exchange networks plays in the life of consumers. This type of information also supports cognitive-behavioural therapeutic approaches, which underline how important it is for participants to break the ties that they have established with their peers in order to attenuate the rationalization and legitimization processes that develop within illicit networks. Holt, Blevins, and Burkert (2010) have shown that simply visiting child-pornography discussion forums during or after treatment reduces the effect of therapy aimed at changing patients' cognition.

But technological advances do not solely benefit child-pornography consumers; they are also very useful to the police in their fight against this type of crime.[1] Just as criminals constantly use the Internet to fulfil their goals, so does law enforcement. The constant progress in international cooperation is also a good sign, as shown, for example, in the arrest by the Sûreté du Québec of twenty-seven suspects on June 25, 2008, with input from German law enforcement agencies,[2] and Operation Salvo in March 2009, during which fifty-seven people were arrested in Canada. The investigation focused on P2P network users who were maintaining a high level of activity on the Gnutella P2P network. Although they are still too few in numbers, units specializing in this type of crime detection are constantly improving their interventions and getting better at detecting child-pornography collectors, given the human and financial resources that they have available.

In this regard, we must emphasize the role of organizations such as Interpol, which is a major facilitator for different police forces around the world, notably in terms of information sharing and the exchange of file signatures (hash values). The setting up and management of a databank of known signature files has made it easier to detect new child-pornography photographs – and to connect them to their producer – and to accelerate identification of new victims in the images. Cooperation and information sharing, as well as the development of new investigation techniques, are central to improving detection of both child-pornography collectors and the children who are central to this illicit trade in cyberspace.

Cooperation among law enforcement agencies and researchers is also essential to refining technical and socio-criminological knowledge in this field. For example, our research on newsgroups has revealed the existence of other virtual sites visited by collectors, as well as the use of new technological tools to obtain illicit content. As they become more familiar with the exchange sites and the relationships established among participants in these networks, police officers will be able to infiltrate new virtual sites that become popular among child-pornography consumers. It is also important for police forces to encourage a more proactive approach by instituting intelligence-led policing and conducting in-depth analyses of the hard disks of arrested consumers and collectors. Police openness to research on and development of new ways of doing things is essential to winning the battle against this type of constantly changing delinquency, even though the anonymity techniques used by collectors and the heavy workload of police officers represent major obstacles.

Unfortunately, child pornography is not an ephemeral phenomenon. We must continue to count on specialized police units around the world, with their specialized training and coordinated efforts, to intervene when such networks are instituted, and on denunciation by Internet users when they discover child-pornography images. It is only as a society that we will be able to limit, as much as possible, the number of these images circulating in cyberspace and, more important still, reduce the number of victims. Detection, information, awareness raising, and education are the keys to winning the fight against child pornography.

Notes

Introduction

1 The Associated Press, January 16, 2014.

2 "Croissance alarmante due trafic," CBC Radio-Canada, www.radio-canada.ca/regions/atlantique/2008/02/12/005-IPE-pornographie.shtml (our translation).

3 *La Presse*, November 15, 2013.

4 Here, we use the terms "pedophilia" and "pedophile" to refer to a psychological disorder in which an adult's principal sexual attraction is to prepubescent children, whether or not there is sexual aggression. We use the expressions "Internet child-pornography collector" and "cyberpedophile" synonymously.

5 "Innocence Exploited: Child Pornography in the Electronic Age," *Canadian Police College*, May 1998.

6 In April 2001, a similar Google search turned up 425,000 results. See www.csec worldcongress.org/PDF/fr/Yokohama/Background_reading/Briefing_notes/Child%20pornography_fr.pdf (no longer active).

7 See also Rainbow Phone (2003).

8 http://www2.ohchr.org/english/bodies/hrcouncil/docs/12session/A.HRC.12.23.pdf.

9 *R v Sharpe*, 2001 SCC 2. [2001] 1 SCR 45, 150 CCC, 321, 39 CR (5th) [*Sharpe*].

10 See Stanley (2001), J. Carr (2004), and Fortin (2005).

11 These technological services are described in greater detail below. Readers may also refer to the glossary in appendix 1 of this book.

12 By "trade," we simply want to suggest that there is a network of child-pornography transactions among a number of social actors who are involved in an exchange process that goes from production to distribution to consumption of illicit materials. This term does not necessarily refer to a monetary exchange of any sort, although this might take place.

Chapter 1: The Investigators and the Law

1 *An Act to amend the Criminal Code (Protection of Children and Other Vulnerable Persons) and the Canada Evidence Act* (S.C. 2005, c. 32).
2 *R. v. Landreville*, 2005 CanLII 60182 (QC C.Q.) – 2005–04–28.
3 The Criminal Code of Canada stipulates that "child pornography" means "a photographic, film, video, or other visual representation, whether or not it was made by electronic or mechanical means," without mentioning that the child portrayed must exist.
4 Particularly what are commonly called manga, anime, and Hentai.
5 In some cases, the children were tied down and the babies were sexually assaulted with tools or other objects.

Chapter 2: The Evolution of ICTs and Their Effect on Trafficking

1 We agree with Wolak, Liberatore, and Levine (2014), who state that they "use the term 'trafficking' because it denotes an illegal trade, which accurately describes the online trade in child pornography. Photographs and videos that contain child pornography are contraband because they show actual children being sexually abused and exploited."
2 According to Taylor (2001, 21), out of the 1,000 child-pornography images that his research group downloaded per week, the majority consisted of older material "such as scans from the old *Lolita* magazines and material that was produced when production and possession of child pornography were legal in a number of European countries about 30 to 40 years ago." See also Wortley and Smallbone (2006); Taylor and Quayle (2003).
3 See also Mitchell, Finkelhor, and Wolak (2005).
4 IRC is "an Internet 'party line' protocol that allows one to converse with others in real time" (Canada Translation Bureau) using a computer keyboard.
5 Another definition is "erotic images of children that do not depict sexually explicit conduct" (www.family.org/socialissues/A000000500.cfm#footnote9).
6 This represents 141,663 queries out of a total of 127,316,861 queries over 70 days in 2007, and 117,621 queries out of a total of 106,344,062 queries over 102 days in 2009.
7 For example, Poulin (2004, 184, 187, our translation), drawing on Rimm (1995), states, "In 1995, kiddie or child porn apparently constituted 48.4% of all downloads from adult web sites" and that in 2003, "The number of known pedophile sites grew by 70%." It must be remembered, however, that this claimed growth of 70% comes from a report by the Italian children's defence association Rainbow Phone and is based on the increase in the number of web sites reported to national and international authorities: 17,016 in 2002.

Chapter 3: How Much Is Out There, and Who Are the Victims?

1 One objective of the COPINE project is to maintain a database on child pornography and evaluate the dangers associated with the collection of child pornography.
2 *Victoria Times Colonist,* April 20, 2007.

3 "Repeat Sex Offender Sentenced to Two Years in Jail," CBC News, September 6, 2001, http://www.oacas.org/news/11/sept/06cp.pdf.
4 See, for instance, a business like Blue Bear, http://www.bb-les.ca/Default.aspx.
5 See National Center for Missing and Exploited Children, http://www.cybertipline.com/home.
6 Ibid., "KeyFacts."
7 *R. v. Beaulieu* CQ: 615–01–011593–061.

Chapter 4: Are Search Engines Enabling?

1 "International Child Porn Ring Smashed," BBC News, March 26, 2001, news.bbc.co.uk/2/hi/americas/1244457.stm.
2 *Le Nouvel Observateur*, June 5, 2003 (our translation).
3 See the NCMEC website, www.missingkids.com. The sociologist Richard Poulin (2004, 187; our translation) states, although he does not discuss the validity of his figures, that "the number of known pedophilic sites on the Internet grew by 70 percent in 2003." According to Poulin's source (the blog <www.blogdei.com>), national and international authorities were notified of 17,016 web sites presenting pornographic scenes involving children in 2002; this number would seem to be low, as, a few pages before (p. 184), he cites a study (Rimm 1995) that states that in 1995, "48.4 percent of all downloads from commercial sites for adults" were linked to child or pseudo-child pornography.
4 See, for instance, Healy (1996); Taylor (1999); Jenkins (2001); Quayle and Taylor (2002); Thornburgh and Lin (2002).
5 "La pornographie enfantine," thematic study presented at the 2nd World Congress against Commercial Sexual Exploitation of Children, held in Yokohama, December 17–20, 2001.
6 See the study *Le commerce de la pédopornographie sur Internet de 2000 à 2010* conducted by Epelboin in 2010. See http://asset.rue89.com/files/business_pedopornographie.pdf.
7 Associated Press, May 6, 2006.
8 See, among others, Verbiest and Wery (2001).
9 For examples, see www.chillingeffects.org/search.cgi?search=pornography.
10 The website PervertedJustice.com, no longer active, claimed, "Contributors to this website are specially trained adult citizens who enter minors' chat rooms to contribute, with the police, to the arrest of adults who sexually solicit children" (our translation). See http://www.perverted-justice.com/.
11 "Google Tackles Child Pornography," BBC News, April 14, 2008, http://news.bbc.co.uk/2/hi/technology/7347476.stm.
12 For more details, see help.Yahoo!.com/l/uk/Yahoo!/info/safety_01.html.
13 See www.cyberaide.ca.
14 A search engine is automated exploration software that "sweeps the network as a whole to index web pages corresponding to the search [formulated]" (Sellier 2003; our translation). Search engines such as Google and Yahoo have revolutionized the field of web searching by enhancing keyword searches with an algorithm called PageRank, which calculates the popularity of sites before ranking them in the search

results (Brin and Page 1999). In other words, the sites that the PageRank algorithm identifies as the most popular may appear first on pages displaying search results.

15 For instance, on the 120 sites listed by the two search engines for the most specific keywords linked to searching for child pornography, only three were found on both lists. Furthermore, twenty of the twenty-six sites listed by Yahoo and Google were listed for the keyword *child porn*, which, as we shall see, generally returns only factual and journalistic information on the subject, but no or very little illicit material per se. We will return to this later in this chapter.

16 The word "porn," rather than "sex," was chosen for the search as it limits the number of educational and general information sites on sexuality returned by the search.

17 Sampling was conducted under conditions controlled by the Sûreté du Québec in order to respect legal boundaries; no child pornography was left on the Sûreté du Québec premises and the researchers never had child pornography in their possession. However, the researchers inevitably had to access child pornography. This access was limited to data collection in order not to contravene paragraph 163.1(4.1) of the Criminal Code of Canada, which stipulates that simply accessing child pornography is an offence.

18 Google states in this regard that the figures it gives are only "an estimate of the total number of search results." See www.google.com/support/webmasters/bin/answer. py?hlrm=en&answer=70920.

19 *R. v. Beaulieu* CQ: 615–01–011593–061.

20 Google asks webmasters to respect certain rules so that the indexing mechanism works properly.

Chapter 5: Are Discussion Forums a Classroom for Cyberpedophiles?

1 In this chapter, we use the expressions "discussion forums" and "newsgroups" interchangeably.

2 O'Connell, a member of the COPINE team, estimates that out of 40,000 discussion forums, 0.07 percent deal explicitly with child pornography. See O'Connell (2001).

3 According to statistics compiled by Altopia.com.

4 A number of newsgroups and articles are added and deleted every day. Also, Usenet exchanges exhibit a time delay – that is, the system is asynchronous and "conversations" do not take place in real time. There is a delay between an initial message being sent and a response being received.

5 "Cyberflics: sq.ca," *Sélection du Reader's Digest*, 637 (2000), 112–20.

6 Initially we studied four discussion forums, but one of them was withdrawn from the analysis because it contained only messages that were encrypted, and therefore illegible. The data-collection period took place between March 17, 2004, and May 1, 2004. For obvious reasons linked to the illegality of these newsgroups, no identifying information making it possible to find them will be included in this book. It should also be noted that we concentrated on "'boy lovers,' as the world of child pornography collectors seems to be sexually stratified: some collectors are interested in young boys, others in young girls, and still others have no gender preference. We wanted to put aside possible biases linked to the question of gender, even though one might imagine that similar interactional dynamics are at work in the different types

of newsgroups" (Corriveau 2010, 385; our translation). Given how quickly technology evolves, it is possible that changes to the parameters of this deviant subculture will occur, such as even more volatile lifespans. Nevertheless, it is unlikely that its internal operations and the elements mentioned here with regard to its formation and composition will disappear.

7 More than 10 gigabytes of information were gathered, or the equivalent of about 7,110 diskettes. All of the messages transmitted were coded, using an analytical checklist in order to create a general and statistical representation of the three newsgroups. To obtain as detailed a description as possible of each group, we first categorized the data collected in terms of the number of participants in each group, the nature of the content exchanged, the scope of these exchanges, and the proportion of the content that was text and binary content (images, video, and so on). Then, these thousands of communications were classified in terms of criteria such as author of the message, his or her IP address (if present), the size of the message sent, the subject covered, the nature of the exchange (text or binary), the presence of attached files, the date and time of the message, and other factors.

8 Several images presented young adults, although they were called "teens."

9 Text messages were sorted into categories previously agreed upon by the researchers. This method of analysis minimizes subjective interpretations as much as possible. First, and without prior consultation with the other members of the team, each researcher analyzed one of the three newsgroups in order to identify the main types of discourse of the users. Only then were the different categories identified by each researcher pooled and compared. We observed that almost all of the categories overlapped.

10 Holt, Blevins, and Burkert (2010, 18) note, "Security is a critical norm within pedophile subculture."

11 In a study of cyber-forums run by and for pedophiles, Holt, Blevins, and Burkert (2010, 18) list the following four safety rules advanced by users who wish to establish an offline relationship: "'1 do not meet until you've had a chance to get to know each other a bit via instant messaging; 2 meet in a neutral place, such as a mall or a restaurant (besides that way there are boys around and you can compare notes); 3 do not surrender phone numbers or addresses until you have already met face to face and get along with this BL.; 4 exercise [sic] common sense.'"

12 We say "almost always" because some images are a montage.

13 According to A. Carr (2004, 31), 22 of the 106 arrested people in his study had used more than one pseudonym.

14 "When an individual offers an excuse, he or she admits that the behavior in question was wrong but denies full responsibility for the act or its consequences. Excuses cite 'circumstances mitigating or entirely eliminating the everyday requirement of accountability'": Rothman and Gandossy (1982, 451), quoted in Durkin and Bryant (1999, 107).

15 This type of excuse seems to be used often as a first defence by people accused of possession of child pornography. See, for instance, *R. v. Beaulieu* CQ: 615–01–011593–061.

16 Durkin and Bryant (1999) note that 39 percent of the cyberpedophiles they studied used this form of argument.

17 See Anonymous, "NAMBLA: The Good News about Man/Boy Love," www.NAMBLA. org (no longer active).

18 According to Richardson and Cialdini (1981, 41), BIRGing consists of "publicly trumpeting some connection with a successful other."

19 Although it is true that this type of custom was socially accepted and not, in general, legally sanctioned, love of youths was strongly supervised by Greek society in order to protect these young citizens. For more details, see Dover (1982), Halperin (2000), and Corriveau (2011).

Chapter 6: Who Are Cyberpedophiles?

1 These numbers were confirmed in 2012 for the province of Quebec: 97 percent were male (and 21 percent of those were minors) (Ministère de la Sécurité publique 2012).

2 Quayle and Taylor (2002) and Jones (1998) also reach this conclusion. As Jones (1998, 58) notes, "Due to increased worldwide legislation, commercial production has diminished ... while not-for-profit production has increased." See also Quayle and Taylor (2003).

3 "Of the 106 offenders sampled, 100 had been involved in Internet-related offences and six had been investigated with regards to objectionable material in the form of video recordings (with two of these also found to be in possession of objectionable photographs, magazines, and letters/stories)" (A. Carr 2004, 25).

4 According to McLaughlin's (2000) study involving 200 defendants, 25 percent were in their twenties, 23.5 percent in their thirties, 26 percent in their forties, 2.5 percent were older than sixty, and 10.5 percent were minors.

5 "The average (mean) age of offenders at the time the offence was investigated was 30 years and the middle (median) age was 28 years" (A. Carr 2004, 31).

6 This research is based on 106 cases studied by A. Carr (2004), to whom were added a further 79 individuals against whom charges had been laid. See also End Child Prostitution and Trafficking (2005).

7 According to A. Carr (2004, 32), the most common age among abusers is seventeen years, with seven defendants.

8 Eighty-one percent of offenders in Wolak, Finkelhor, and Mitchell's (2005) sample were full-time employees.

9 Of the 112 defendants with a criminal record, "24% of the sample had prior contact sexual offenses, 17% had prior noncontact sexual offenses, and 15% had prior child pornography offenses" – that is, almost 63 defendants out of the 201 individuals in the sample (Seto and Eke 2005).

10 See Wortley and Smallbone (2006); Alexy, Burgess, and Baker (2005); Krone (2005); End Child Prostitution and Trafficking (2005); Wolak, Finkelhor, and Mitchell (2005); Middleton, Beech, and Mandeville-Norden (2005).

11 The idea of the continuum is highlighted in Middleton, Beech, and Mandeville-Norden (2005, 106): "The research supports the suggestion that men who use the Internet to obtain indecent images of children are not a homogeneous group. With the addition of more cases for analysis it may be that these offenders can be placed along a continuum. These would range from low risk, low deviance offenders who

are unlikely to pursue their sexual interests into 'contact' offences at one extreme, to those offenders who are high risk and high deviance who display many of the pre-disposing attitudes and behavior supportive of serial abuse."

12 Generally, cyberpedophiles try to establish a friendship with the young person, while ensuring, by sending photographs for example, that they are actually communicating with a young person and not a police officer or other adult. As conversation continues, the groomer will suggest to the young person that they continue their discussion via some other medium, preferably by email, instant messaging, or with the assistance of a webcam. Once he has reached this crucial point, the cyberpedophile assesses the risk of being caught by an adult by finding out whether the young person is using a personal computer, is in his or her room, and so on. If the answers are satisfactory, he tries to gain the trust of the young person by talking about kissing, caressing, masturbation, and, eventually, sexual intercourse. See also Action Innocence (2008), J. Carr (2004), Berson (2003), and O'Connell (2003).

Conclusion

1 For instance, the software called LACE developed by BlueBear, a company based in the province of Quebec, facilitates police analysis of defendants' computers.
2 Canadian Press, Thursday, June 26, 2008.

References

Abel, G.G., J.V. Becker, and J. Cunningham-Rathner. 1984. "Complications, Consent, and Cognitions in Sex between Children and Adults." *International Journal of Law and Psychiatry* 7 (1): 89–103. http://dx.doi.org/10.1016/0160-2527(84)90008-6.

Action Innocence. 2008. *Le mode opératoire du Cyber pédophile: Analyse de 6 cas de Suisse Romande*. Geneva: Action Innocence.

Alexy, E.M., A.W. Burgess, and T. Baker. 2005. "Internet Offenders: Traders, Travelers, and Combination Trader/Travelers." *Journal of Interpersonal Violence* 20 (7): 804–12. http://dx.doi.org/10.1177/0886260505276091.

Armagh, D., N. Battaglia, and K. Lanning. 1999. *Use of Computers in the Sexual Exploitation of Children*. Washington, DC: US Department of Justice.

Åström, P.-E. 2004. *Child Pornography on the Internet: Beyond All Tolerance – A Growing Problem Demanding New Counter-Measures*. Save the Children Sweden. http://resourcecentre.savethechildren.se/sites/default/files/documents/2476.pdf.

AuCoin, Kathy. 2005. "Children and Youth as Victims of Violent Crime." *Juristat* 25 (1). Statistics Canada Catalogue no. 85–002-XIE.

Babchishin, K.M., K.R. Hanson, and C.A. Hermann. 2011. "The Characteristics of Online Sex Offenders: A Meta-Analysis." *Sexual Abuse: a Journal of Research and Treatment* 23 (1): 92–123. doi:10.1177/1079063210370708.

Badgley, R. 1984. *Sexual Offences against Children*. Ottawa: Canadian Government Publishing Centre.

Becker, Howard S. 1963. *Outsiders: Studies in the Sociology of Deviance*. New York: Free Press of Glencoe.

Belk, R.W. 1995. "Collecting as Luxury Consumption: Effects on Individuals and Households." *Journal of Economic Psychology* 16 (3): 477–90. http://dx.doi.org/10.1016/0167-4870(95)98956-X.

Berberi, S., S. Boulanger, F. Fortin, D. Maleza, G. Ouellet, J. Paquin, and S. Rodrigue. 2003. *La cybercriminalité au Québec*. Ministère de la Sécurité publique, strategic analysis report, 50–77. Montreal: Sûreté du Québec, Service du renseignement criminel.

Berson, I.R. 2003. "Grooming Cybervictims: The Psychosocial Effects of Online Exploitation for Youth." *Journal of School Violence* 2 (1): 5–18. http://dx.doi.org/10.1300/J202v02n01_02.

Bourke, M.L., and A.E. Hernandez. 2009. "The "Butner Redux": A Report of the Incidence of Hands-On Child Victimization by Child Pornography Offenders." *Journal of Family Violence* 24 (3): 183–91. http://dx.doi.org/10.1007/s10896-008-9219-y.

Brin, S., and L. Page. 1999. The Anatomy of a Large-Scale Hypertextual Web Search Engine. *Computer Networks* 30 (1–7): 107–17.

Bunzeluk, Kelly. 2009. *Child Sexual Abuse Images: An Analysis of Websites by Cybertip.ca*. Winnipeg: Canadian Centre for Child Protection.

Burgess, A.W., and M.L. Clark, eds. 1984. *Child Pornography and Sex Rings*. New York: Lexington Books.

Burgess, A.W., and C.R. Hartman. 1987. "Child Abuse Aspects of Child Pornography." *Psychiatric Annals* 17 (4): 248–53. http://dx.doi.org/10.3928/0048-5713-19870401-08.

Carlstedt, A., T. Nilsson, B. Hofvander, A. Brimse, S. Innala, and H. Anckarsater. 2009. "Does Victim Age Differentiate between Perpetrators of Sexual Child Abuse? A Study of Mental Health, Psychosocial Circumstances, and Crimes." *Sexual Abuse: A Journal of Research and Treatment* 21 (4): 442–54. doi:10.1177/1079063209346699.

Carr, A. 2004. *Internet Traders of Child Pornography and Other Censorship Offenders in New Zealand*. Wellington: Department of Internal Affairs Te Tari Taiwhenua.

Carr, J. 2001. "La pornographie enfantine." Paper presented at "2nd World Congress against Commercial Sexual Exploitation of Children," Yokohama, December 17–20.

–. 2004. *Child Abuse, Child Pornography and the Internet*. London: NCH.

Corriveau, Patrice. 2010. "Les groupes de nouvelles à caractère pédopornographique: Une sous-culture de la déviance." *Déviance et Société* 34 (3): 381–400. http://dx.doi.org/10.3917/ds.343.0381.

–. 2011. *Judging Homosexuals: A History of Gay Persecution in Quebec and France*. Vancouver: UBC Press.

Crewdson, J. 1988. *By Silence Betrayed: Sexual Abuse of Children in America*. Boston: Little Brown.

Cronin, B., and E. Davenport. 2001. "E-Rogenous Zones: Positioning Pornography in the Digital Economy." *Information Society* 17 (1): 33–48. http://dx.doi.org/10.1080/019722401750067414.

Demetriou, C., and A. Silke. 2003. "A Criminological 'Sting': Experimental Evidence of Illegal and Deviant Visits to a Website Trap." *British Journal of Criminology* 43 (1): 213–22. http://dx.doi.org/10.1093/bjc/43.1.213.

Dobson, A. 2003, 13 February. Caught in the Net. *Care and Health*, 6–9.

Dover, K.J. 1982. *L'homosexualité grecque.* Paris: La Découverte.

Durkin, K.F., and C.D. Bryant. 1999. "Propagandizing Pederasty: A Thematic Analysis of the On-line Exculpatory Accounts of Unrepentant Pedophiles." *Deviant Behavior: An Interdisciplinary Journal* 20 (2): 103–27. http://dx.doi.org/10.1080/016396299266524.

End Child Prostitution and Trafficking. 2002. *Child Pornography: Frequently Asked Questions about Commercial Sexual Exploitation of Children.* www.ecpat.net/eng.

–. 2005. *Violence against Children in Cyberspace: A Contribution to the United Nations Study on Violence against Children.* Bangkok: ECPAT.

Ferreday, D. 2003. "Unspeakable Bodies: Erasure, Embodiment and the Pro-Ana Community." *International Journal of Cultural Studies* 6 (3): 277–95. http://dx.doi.org/10.1177/13678779030063003.

Fillieule, R., and C. Montiel. 1997. *La pédophilie.* Paris: Institut des hautes études de la sécurité intérieure.

Fontana-Rosa, J. 2001. "Legal Competency in a Case of Pedophilia: Advertising on the Internet." *International Journal of Offender Therapy and Comparative Criminology* 45 (1): 118–28. http://dx.doi.org/10.1177/0306624X0145 1008.

Forde, P., and A. Patterson. 1998. "Paedophiles Internet Activity." *Trends and Issues in Crime and Criminal Justice* 97: 1–6.

Fortin, F. 2005. *Criminalité informatique: Un survol des tendances en évolution.* Presentation at the Congrès de la Société de criminologie du Québec, Sainte-Adèle, 25–27 May.

–. 2014. "C'est ma collection mais c'est bien plus que ça: Analyse des processus de collecte et de l'évolution des images dans les collections de pornographie juvénile." PhD diss., University of Montreal.

Fortin, F., and P. Corriveau. 2013. "Pornographie juvénile et intervention policière." In *Cybercriminalité: Entre inconduite et crime organisé,* ed. F. Fortin, 366. Montreal: Presses Internationales Polytechnique.

Fortin, F., and S. Lapointe. 2002. Internet qu'est-ce que ça change? Usages problématiques et criminels d'Internet. Paper presented at the Congrès de l'Association des médecins psychiatres, Mont-Tremblant, June 7.

Fortin, F., and J. Roy. 2006. "Profils des consommateurs de pornographie juvénile arrêtés au Québec: L'explorateur, le pervers et le polymorphe." *Criminologie* 39 (1): 107–28. http://dx.doi.org/10.7202/013128ar.

–. 2007. "Cyberpédophilie: Profiles d'amateur de pédopornographie" [Cyberpedophilia: Profiles of users of child pornography]. In *Psychologie des entrevues d'enquête: De la recherche à la pratique* [From research to practice: The psychology of investigative interviews], ed. M. St-Yves and M. Tanguay, 465–502. Montreal: Éditions Yvon Blais.

Frank, R., B. Westlake, and M. Bouchard. 2010. "The Structure and Content of Online Child Exploitation Networks." Paper presented at the ACM SIGKDD Workshop on Intelligence and Security Informatics, Washington, DC.

Friedman, N.L. 1974. "Cookies and Contests: Notes on Ordinary Occupational Deviance and Its Neutralization." *Sociological Symposium* 11: 1–9.

Gagnon, B. 2007. "Les technologies de l'information et le terrorisme." In *Repenser le terrorisme, concepts, acteurs et réponses*, ed. C.-P. David and B. Gagnon, 243–70. Quebec City: Presses de l'Université Laval.

Gakenback, J. 1998. *Psychology of the Internet: Intrapersonal, Interpersonal, and Transpersonal Implications*. London: Academic Press.

Gaspar, R., and P.C. Bibby. 1996. "How Rings Work." In *Organized Abuse: The Current Debate*, ed. P.C. Bibby. Brookfield, VT: Ashgate.

Gendarmerie royale du Canada. 1994. "La pornographie enfantine." *La Gazette de la GRC* 56 (9): 20–22.

General Accounting Office. 2003, February. *File-Sharing Programs. Peer-to-Peer Networks Provide Ready Access to Child Pornography*. Washington, DC: United States General Accounting Office.

Gough, D. 1993. *Child Abuse Interventions: A Review of the Research Literature*. London: HMSO.

Guttman, C. 1999. "Internet et la pédophilie." *Le Courrier de l'Unesco*. http://www.unesco.org/new/fr/unesco-courier/.

Halperin, D. 2000. *Cent ans d'homosexualité et autres essais sur l'amour grec*. Paris: EPEL.

Hames, M. 1993. "Child Pornography: A Secret Web of Exploitation." *Child Abuse Review* 2 (4): 276–80. http://dx.doi.org/10.1002/car.2380020410.

Hanson, R.K., and H. Scott. 1996. "Social Networks of Sexual Offenders." *Psychology, Crime and Law* 2 (4): 249–58. http://dx.doi.org/10.1080/10683169608409782.

Harmon, D., and S.B. Boeringer. 1997. "A Content Analysis of Internet-Accessible Written Pornographic Depictions." *Electronic Journal of Sociology* 3 (1): http://sociology.org/content/vol003.001/boeringer.html.

Hartman, C.R., A.W. Burgess, and K.V. Lanning. 1984. "Typology of Collectors." In *Child Pornography and Sex Rings*, ed. A.W. Burgess, 93–109. Lexington, MA: Lexington Books.

Healy, M.A. 1996. *Child Pornography: An International Perspective*. Stockholm: World Congress Against Commercial Sexual Exploitation of Children.

Holmes, R.M., and S.T. Holmes. 2002. *Sex Crimes: Pattern and Behavior*. Thousand Oaks: Sage Publications.

Holt, T.J., K.R. Blevins, and N. Burkert. 2010. "Considering the Pedophile Subculture Online." *Sexual Abuse* 22 (1): 3–24. doi:10.1177/1079063209344979.

Howitt, D. 1995. *Paedophiles and Sexual Offences against Children*. Chichester: J. Wiley.

Iacub, M. 2010. *De la pornographie en Amérique: La liberté de la démocratie deliberative*. Paris: Fayard.

International Save the Children Alliance. 2005. "Position Paper Regarding Online Images of Sexual Abuse and Other Internet-Related Sexual Exploitation of Children." Save the Children Sweden. http://resourcecentre.savethechildren.se/sites/default/files/documents/1782.pdf.

Jenkins, P. 2001. *Beyond Tolerance: Child Pornography Online*. New York: New York University Press.

Johnson, K. 2001. "100 Arrested in Net Child Porn Crackdown." *USA Today*, http://usatoday30.usatoday.com/tech/news/2001-08-08-child-porn.htm.

Jones, L.M. 1998. "Regulating Child Pornography on the Internet: The Implications of Article 34 of the United Nations Convention of the Rights of the Child." *International Journal of Children's Rights* 6 (1): 55–79. http://dx.doi.org/10.1163/15718189820493978.

Jordan, T., and P. Taylor. 1998. "A Sociology of Hackers." *Sociological Review* 46 (4): 757–80. http://dx.doi.org/10.1111/1467-954X.00139.

Kelly, L. 1992. "Pornography and Child Sexual Abuse." In *Pornography: Women, Violence and Civil Liberties*, ed. C. Itzen, 113–23. Oxford: Oxford University Press.

Khan, K. 2000. "Child Pornography on the Internet." *Police Journal* 73 (1): 7–17.

Klain, E.J., H.J. Davies, and M.A. Hicks. 2001. *Child Pornography: The Criminal-Justice-System Response*. Report no. NC81. Alexandria, VA: American Bar Association Center on Children and the Law.

Kong, R., H. Johnson, S. Beattie, and A. Cardillo. 2003. "Sexual Offences in Canada." *Juristat* 23 (6), catalogue 85–002.

Krone, T. 2004. "A Typology of Online Child Pornography Offending." *Trends and Issues in Crime and Criminal Justice* 279, July. http://aic.gov.au/media_library/publications/tandi2/tandi279.pdf.

–. 2005. "Does Thinking Make It So? Defining Online Child Pornography Possession Offences." *Trends and Issues in Crime and Criminal Justice* 299, April. http://aic.gov.au/media_library/publications/tandi/tandi299.pdf .

Langevin, R., R.A. Lang, P. Wright, L. Handy, Roy R. Frenzel, and Edward L. Black. 1988. "Pornography and Sexual Offences." *Annals of Sex Research* 1 (3): 335–62. http://dx.doi.org/10.1007/BF00878103.

Lanning, K.V. 1984. "Collectors." In *Child Pornography and Sex Rings*, ed. A.W. Burgess and M.L. Clark, 83–109. Lexington, MA: Lexington Books.

–. 1992. *Child Molesters: A Behavioural Analysis*. Washington, DC: National Center for Missing and Exploited Children.

Lanning, K.V., and A.W. Burgess. 1989. "Child Pornography and Sex Rings." In *Pornography: Research Advances and Policy Considerations*, ed. D. Zillman and J. Bryant, 235–58. Hillsdale: Lawrence Erlbaum.

Legardinier, C. 2002. *Les trafics du sexe: Femmes et enfants marchandises*. Toulouse: Éditions Milan.

Le Grand, B., J.-L. Guillaume, M. Latapy, and C. Magnien, C. 2010. "Dynamics of Paedophile Keywords in *eDonkey* Queries." http://antipaedo.lip6.fr/T24/TR/kw-dynamics.pdf.

Lesce, T. 1999. "Law Enforcement Investigates Abuse." *Law and Order* 47 (5): 74–78.

Levesque, R. 1999. *Sexual Abuse of Children: A Human Rights Perspective*. Bloomington: Indiana University Press.

Levy, N. 2002. "Virtual Child Pornography: The Eroticization of Inequality." *Ethics and Information Technology* 4 (4): 319–23. http://dx.doi.org/10.1023/A:1021372601566.

Liberatore, M., R. Erdely, T. Kerle, B.N. Levine, and C. Shields. 2010. "Forensic Investigation of Peer-to-Peer File Sharing Networks." *Digital Investigation* 7(S): S95–S103. doi:10.1016/j.diin.2010.05.012.

Lööf, L. 2005. "Global Issues and Regional Co-operation Fighting Child Exploitation." In *Viewing Child Pornography on the Internet: Understanding the Offence,*

Managing the Offender, Helping the Victims, ed. E. Quayle and M. Taylor, 151–60. London: Russell House Publishing.

Loughlin, J., and A. Taylor-Butts. 2009. "Child Luring through the Internet." *Juristat* 29 (1): http://www.statcan.gc.ca/pub/85-002-x/2009001/article/10783-eng.pdf.

Magaletta, P.R., E. Faust, W. Bickart, and A.M. McLearen. 2014. "Exploring Clinical and Personality Characteristics of Adult Male Internet-Only Child Pornography Offenders." *International Journal of Offender Therapy and Comparative Criminology* 58 (2): 137–53. http://dx.doi.org/10.1177/0306624X12465271.

Make-It-Safe. 2005. "First Case of Child-Porn Cartoons." Make-It Safe, "In the News," October 20. www.make-it-safe.net/eng/news_archives/2005_10_20_01.asp.

Mayer, A. 1985. *Sexual Abuse: Causes, Consequences and Treatment of Incestuous and Pedophilic Acts*. Holmes Beach, FL: Learning.

McAndrew, D. 1999. "The Structural Analysis of Criminal Networks." In *The Social Psychology of Crime: Groups, Teams, and Networks, Offender Profiling Series*, ed. D. Canter and L. Alison, 53–94. Dartmouth: Aldershot.

McLaughlin, J.F. 2000. *Cyber Child Sex Offender Typology*. www.ci.keene.nh.us/police/Typology.html.

McWhaw, A. 2011. "Online Child Pornography Offenders and Risk Assessment: How Online Offenders Compare to Contact Offenders Using Common Risk Assessment Variables." PhD diss., University of Ottawa.

Merdian, H., N. Wilson, and D.P. Boer. 2009. "Characteristics of Internet Sexual Offenders: A Review." *Sexual Abuse in Australia and New Zealand: An Interdisciplinary Journal* 2 (1): 34–47.

Middleton, D., A. Beech, and R. Mandeville-Norden. 2005. "What Sort of Person Could Do That? Psychological Profiles of Internet Pornography Users." In *Viewing Child Pornography on the Internet: Understanding the Offence, Managing the Offender, Helping the Victims*, ed. E. Quayle and M. Taylor, 99–107. London: Russell House Publishing.

Ministère de la Sécurité publique du Québec. 2007. "Police et sécurité privée: Les six niveaux de services." http://www.securitepublique.gouv.qc.ca/police/police-quebec/services-police/desserte-policiere/six-niveaux-service.html.

–. 2012. "Infractions sexuelles au Québec: Faits saillants 2012." http://www.securitepublique.gouv.qc.ca/fileadmin/Documents/statistiques/agressions_sexuelles/2012/agressions_sexuelles_2012.pdf.

Mitchell, K.J., D. Finkelhor, and J. Wolak. 2005. "The Internet and Family and Acquaintance Sexual Abuse." *Child Maltreatment* 10 (1): 49–60. http://dx.doi.org/10.1177/1077559504271917.

Mitchell, K.J., J. Wolak, and D. Finkelhor. 2005. "Police Posing as Juveniles Online to Catch Sex Offenders: Is It Working?" *Sexual Abuse: A Journal of Research and Treatment* 17 (3): 241–67. doi:10.1177/107906320501700302.

Muensterberger, W. 1994. *Collecting: An Unruly Passion*. Princeton: Princeton University Press.

Nathenson, I.S. 1998. "Internet Infoglut and Invisible Ink: Spamdexing Search Engines with Meta Tags." *Harvard Journal of Law and Technology* 12 (1). http://papers.ssrn.com/sol3/papers.cfm?abstract_id=1469706.

National Center for Missing and Exploited Children. 2006. *2006 Amber Alert Report.* www.missingkids.com.

National Clearinghouse on Family Violence. 2006. *Child Sexual Abuse.* Ottawa: Government of Canada.

O'Connell, R. 2001. "Paedophiles Networking on the Internet." In *Child Abuse on the Internet: Ending the Silence,* ed. C.A. Arnaldo, 65–79. Paris: Berghahn Books and UNESCO.

—. 2003. *A Typology of Cybersexploitation and On-Line Grooming Practices.* Preston, UK: University of Central Lancashire, Cyberspace Research Unit.

O'Halloran, E., and E. Quayle. 2010. "A Content Analysis of a 'Boy Love' Support Forum: Revisiting Durkin and Bryant." *Journal of Sexual Aggression* 16 (1): 71–85. http://dx.doi.org/10.1080/13552600903395319.

Ouellet, I. 2008. "Exploitation sexuelle des enfants sur Internet." Paper presented at "L'intersectoriel, pour des actions réalistes et efficaces auprès des victimes d'agression sexuelle, Québec," Quebec City, November.

Palmer, T. 2005. "Behind the Screen: Children Who Are the Subjects of Abusive Images." In *Viewing Child Pornography on the Internet: Understanding the Offence, Managing the Offender, Helping the Victims,* ed. E. Quayle and M. Taylor, 61–74. London: Russell House Publishing.

Perez, L.M., J. Jones, D.R. Englert, and D. Sachau. 2010. "Secondary Traumatic Stress and Burnout among Law Enforcement Investigators Exposed to Disturbing Media Images." *Journal of Police and Criminal Psychology* 25 (2): 113–24. doi:10.1007/s11896-010-9066-7.

Poulin, R. 2004. *La mondialisation des industries du sexe: Prostitution, pornographie, traite des femmes et des enfants.* Ottawa: Les Éditions L'Interligne.

Preece, J. 2000. *Online Communities: Designing Usability and Supporting Sociability.* New York: John Wiley and Sons.

Prichard, Jeremy, Paul A. Watters, and Caroline Spiranovic. 2011. "Internet Subcultures and Pathways to the Use of Child Pornography." *Computer Law and Security Report* 27 (6): 585–600. http://dx.doi.org/10.1016/j.clsr.2011.09.009.

Quayle, Esther, and Terry Jones. 2011. "Sexualized Images of Children on the Internet," *Sexual Abuse: A Journal of Research and Treatment* 23 (1): 7–21.

Quayle, E., and M. Taylor. 2002. "Paedophiles, Pornography and the Internet: Assessment Issues." *British Journal of Social Work* 32 (7): 863–75. http://dx.doi.org/10.1093/bjsw/32.7.863.

—. 2003. "Model of Problematic Internet Use in People with a Sexual Interest in Children." *Cyberpsychology and Behavior* 6 (1): 93–106. http://dx.doi.org/10.1089/109493103321168009.

Rainbow Phone (Telefono Arcobaleno). 2003. *Monitoring of Pedophilia Online: Annual Report.* Rainbow Phone Association.

Rettinger, L.J. 2000. *La relation entre la pornographie juvénile et les infractions sexuelles contre les enfants: Une analyse documentaire.* Ottawa: Ministère de la Justice du Canada.

Richardson, K., and R.B. Cialdini. 1981. "Basking and Blasting: Tactics of Indirect Self-Presentation." In *Impression Management Theory and Social Psychological*

Research, ed. J.T. Tedeschi, 41–53. New York: Academic Press. http://dx.doi. org/10.1016/B978-0-12-685180-9.50008-7.

Rimer, Jonah. 2007. *Literature Review: Responding to Child and Youth Victims of Sexual Exploitation on the Internet, 2007.* http://www.boostforkids.org/pdf/ RCE-Literature-Review.pdf (no longer active).

Rimm, M. 1995. "Marketing Pornography on the Information Superhighway." *Georgetown Law Journal* 83: 1849–934.

Rothman, M.L., and R.P. Gandossy. 1982. "Sad Tale: The Accounts of White-Collar Defendants and the Decision to Sanction." *Pacific Sociological Review* 25 (4): 449–73. http://dx.doi.org/10.2307/1388924.

Roy, J. 2004. "Étude exploratoire des événements et des caractéristiques des individus mis en cause dans des cas de possession et de distribution de matériel pornographique juvénile sur Internet." Unpublished internship report, École de criminologie, Université de Montréal, Montreal.

Savary, C. 2005. "La Couronne réclame 15 mois de prison ferme contre André Von Gunten: L'accusé a été trouvé en possession de 44 000 photos de pornographie juvénile." *Le Nouvelliste* 23 (April): 3.

Schell, B.H., M.V. Martin, P.C.K. Hung, and L. Rueda. 2007. "Cyber Child Pornography: A Review Paper of the Social and Legal Issues and Remedies — and a Proposed Technological Solution." *Aggression and Violent Behavior* 12 (1): 45–63. http://dx.doi.org/10.1016/j.avb.2006.03.003.

Scott, M.B., and S. Lyman. 1968. "Accounts." *American Sociological Review* 33 (1): 46–62. http://dx.doi.org/10.2307/2092239.

Sellier, H. 2003. *Innocence-en-danger.com: Internet – Le paradis des pédophiles.* Paris: Éditions Plon.

Seto, M.C. 2008. *Pedophilia and Sexual Offending against Children: Theory, Assessment, and Intervention.* Washington, DC: American Psychological Association. http://dx.doi.org/10.1037/11639-000.

–. 2009. "Pedophilia." *Annual Review of Clinical Psychology* 5 (1): 391–407. http:// dx.doi.org/10.1146/annurev.clinpsy.032408.153618.

Seto, M.C., and A. Eke. 2005. "Criminal Histories and Later Offending of Child Pornography Offenders." *Sexual Abuse* 17: 201–10.

Skoog, D.M., and J.L. Murray. 1998. *Innocence Exploited: Child Pornography in the Electronic Age.* Canadian Police College and University of Winnipeg.

Smallbone, S., and R. Wortley. 2000. *Child Sexual Abuse in Queensland: Offender Characteristics and Modus Operandi.* Brisbane: Queensland Crime Commission.

Sohier, D.J. 1998. *Internet: Le guide de l'internaute 1998.* Montreal: Éditions Logiques.

Stanley, J. 2001. "Child Abuse and the Internet." *National Child Protection Clearinghouse* 15 (Summer): 1–18.

Steel, C.M.S. 2009a. "Child Pornography in Peer-to-Peer Networks." *Child Abuse and Neglect* 33 (8): 560–68. doi:10.1016/j.chiabu.2008.12.011.

–. 2009b. "Web-Based Child Pornography." *International Journal of Digital Crime and Forensics* 1 (4): 58–69. doi:10.4018/jdcf.2009062405.

Strano, M. 2003. "Analisi criminological e profiling dei pedofili on-line." *Telematic Journal of Clinical Criminology.* International Crime Analysis Association.

www.vertici.com/rubriche/articolo.asp?cod=9179&cat=STUDI&titlepage=St udi%20e%20ricerche.

Sykes, G., and D. Matza. 1957. "Techniques of Neutralization: A Theory of Delinquency." *American Sociological Review* 22 (6): 664–70. http://dx.doi.org/10.2307/2089195.

Tate, T. 1990. *Child Pornography: An Investigation*. London: Methuen.

—. 1992. "The Child Pornography Industry: International Trade in Child Sexual Abuse." In *Pornography: Women, Violence and Civil Liberties*, ed. C. Itzen, 203–16. Oxford: Oxford University Press.

Taylor, M. 1999. "The Nature and Dimensions of Child Pornography on the Internet." Paper presented at "Combating Child Pornography on the Internet Conference," Vienna, September 29 to October 1.

—. 2001. Rethinking the Line: The Canada-U.S. Border, Child Pornography on the Internet Session. Department of Justice Canada, Research and Statistics Division, report of conference held October 22, 2000, Vancouver, British Columbia. http://www.justice.gc.ca/eng/rp-pr/other-autre/op01_20-po01_20/op01_20. pdf.

Taylor, M., G. Holland, and E. Quayle. 2001. "Typology of Paedophile Picture Collections." *Police Journal* 74 (2): 97–107.

Taylor, M., and E. Quayle. 2003. *Child Pornography: An Internet Crime*. New York: Routledge.

Taylor, M., E. Quayle, and G. Holland. 2001. "La pornographie infantile, l'Internet et les comportements délinquants." *Isuma: Canadian Journal of Policy Research* 2 (2): 1–12.

Temporini, H. 2012. "Child Pornography and the Internet." *Psychiatric Clinics of NA* 35 (4): 821–35. doi:10.1016/j.psc.2012.08.004.

Thornberry, T. 1987. "Towards an Interactional Theory of Delinquency." *Criminology* 25 (4): 863–92. http://dx.doi.org/10.1111/j.1745-9125.1987.tb00823.x.

Thornburgh, D., and H. Lin, eds. 2002. *Youth, Pornography and the Internet*. Washington, DC: National Academy Press.

Tremblay, P. 2002. *Social Interactions among Paedophiles*. Cahiers de recherches criminologiques, no. 36. Montreal: Université de Montréal, Centre international de criminologie comparée.

Verbiest, T., and E. Wery. 2001. *Le droit de l'Internet et de la société de l'information: Droits européens, belges et français*. Brussels: Éditions Laurcier, Création Information Communication imprint.

Warren, J.I., P.E. Dietz, and R.R. Hazelwood. 2013. "The Collectors: Serial Sexual Offenders Who Preserve Evidence of Their Crimes." *Aggression and Violent Behavior* 18 (6): 666–72. http://dx.doi.org/10.1016/j.avb.2013.07.020.

Wellard, S.S. 2001. "Cause and Effect." *Community Care*, March 15-21, 26–27.

Wolak, J., D. Finkelhor, and K.J. Mitchell. 2003. "Internet Sex Crimes against Minors: The Response of Law Enforcement." http://www.unh.edu/ccrc/pdf/jvq/CV70.pdf.

—. 2005. *Child-Pornography Possessors Arrested in Internet-Related Crimes*. National Center for Missing and Exploited Children. http://www.missingkids.com/en_US/publications/NC144.pdf

–. 2011. "Child Pornography Possessors: Trends in Offender and Case Characteristics." *Sexual Abuse: A Journal of Research and Treatment* 23 (1): 22–42. doi:10.1177/1079063210372143.

–. 2012. "Trends in Arrests for Child Pornography Production: The Third National Juvenile Online Victimization Study." NJOV-3. Durham, NH: Crimes against Children Research Center.

Wolak, J., M. Liberatore, and B.N. Levine. 2014. "Measuring a Year of Child Pornography Trafficking by U.S. Computers on a Peer-to-peer Network." *Child Abuse & Neglect* 38 (2): 347–56. http://dx.doi.org/10.1016/j.chiabu.2013.10.018.

Wortley, R., and S. Smallbone. 2006. *Child Pornography on the Internet: Problem-Oriented Guides for Police*. US Department of Justice.

Wyre, R. 1992. "Pornography and Sexual Violence: Working with Sex Offenders." In *Pornography: Women, Violence and Civil Liberties*, ed. C. Itzen, 237–47. Oxford: Oxford University Press.

Zook, M.A. 2003. "Underground Globalization: Mapping the Space of Flows of the Internet Adult Industry." *Environment & Planning* 35 (7): 1261–86. http://dx.doi.org/10.1068/a35105.

Index

79–80, 91*n*3, 94*n*2; content of, 5,
26–30, 36–42; discussion forums/
newsgroups and, 4, 6, 20, 22, 43–65;
ICTs and, 4, 5, 13–22, 86–88; as
increasingly "homemade," 30;
legislation governing, 3–4, 8–12, 22,
90*n*3, 92*n*17; media coverage of, 1–3;
and profiles of collectors, 6, 66–85;
quantity of, 5, 23–26; Quebec police
unit targeting, 4, 5, 7–8, 17; search
engines and, 5–6, 31–42; and sex
tourism, 30; and sexual abuse/assault,
2, 15–16, 26–27, 30, 43–44, 62–63,
66, 69–85; as unlikely to be found on
web, 20, 22, 33, 39–42; victims of, 5,
28–30. *See also specific topics*
child cyberpornography collectors, 6,
66–85; in Canada and abroad, 70–72,
72(t); categories/types of, 68–70,
76–80, 81(f); common traits among,
73–76; criminal records of, 67–70,
71–73; as educated professionals, 71,
72; and link between collecting and
abuse, 66, 82–85; in Quebec, 67–70,
71, 72(t); sociodemographic profile
of, 66, 68–73; typological synthesis
of, 80–85. *See also entries below*;
arrests, of child cyberpornography
collectors; deviant communities, of
child cyberpornography collectors,
and entry following
child cyberpornography collectors, as
abusers: categories/types of, 69–70,
77, 78, 79–80, 81(f), 82; examples
of, 69–70, 83; and link between
collecting and abuse, 66, 82–85; value
of images for, 75–76
child cyberpornography collectors,
categories/types of, 68–70, 76–80;
as collector-abuser, 66, 69–70, 71,
75–76, 77, 78, 79–80, 82–85; as
collector-distributor, 68–69, 77, 78,
80; as "collector in passing," 80; as
collector only, 68, 76–77, 78, 80;
diagram of, 81(f)

child cyberpornography collectors,
in Quebec: and age at arrest,
72(t); categories/types of, 68–70;
demographics/criminal records
of, 67–68, 70, 71; students/jobless
among, 67
Child Exploitation and Online Protection
Centre (UK), 32; ChildBase of, 2
child pornography: in comic book/
animated form, 12; evolution of
trafficking in, 13–14; as homemade,
14; in Internet era, 14–15; legal
definitions of, 8–11, 90*n*3; in
magazines, 13, 15, 45, 73, 90*n*2, 94*n*3;
and sex tourism, 30; on videotape,
14, 15, 45, 73. *See also* child
cyberpornography
Child Pornography Prevention Act
(US), 12
collectors. *See* child cyberpornography
collectors, *and entries following*
commercial child pornography
websites, 20, 31–32, 68, 70, 91*n*3
commercial/financial motivation, of
participants in trafficking, 70, 77,
79–80, 94*n*2
communities, online. *See*
deviant communities, of child
cyberpornography collectors, *and
entry following*
compressed (zip) files, 20–21, 25
content of child cyberpornography,
in COPINE databank, 26–30; and
classification of images, 26–28; and
demographics (sex, age, ethnicity) of
victims, 28–30. *See also entry below*;
COPINE
content of websites, as found in
authors' search engine study, 36–38,
39(t); adult pornography (with/
without images), 37–38, 39(t);
child pornography (with/without
images), 37, 38, 39(t); information
(anti-pornography), 36; invalid
(defunct website), 36, 39(t); "other"

Printed and bound in Canada by Friesens

Set in Segoe and Warnock by Apex CoVantage, LLC

Copy editor: Steven Sacks

Proofreader: Jillian Shoichet

Indexer: Cheryl Lemmens